JOOKIN'

JOOKIN'

THE RISE OF
SOCIAL DANCE FORMATIONS
IN AFRICAN-AMERICAN
CULTURE

Katrina Hazzard-Gordon

TEMPLE UNIVERSITY PRESS ■ PHILADELPHIA

Temple University Press, Philadelphia 19122
Copyright © 1990 by Temple University. All rights reserved
Published 1990
Printed in the United States of America

The paper used in this publication meets the minimum
requirements of American National Standard for Information
Sciences—Permanence of Paper for Printed Library Materials,
ANSI Z39.48-1984

Library of Congress Cataloging-in-Publication Data
Hazzard-Gordon, Katrina.
Jookin' : the rise of social dance formations in African-American
culture / Katrina Hazzard-Gordon.
p.   cm.
Bibliography: p.
Includes index.
ISBN 0-87722-613-X (alk. paper)
1. Afro-Americans—Dancing—History.   I. Title.
GV1624.7.A34H39   1990
793.3089'96073—dc20   89-32004
                                                              CIP

For the forgotten jook-house participants,
for my family—
Susie, Stonewall, Honey-baby, Jimmy and Jameka—
and for Africans everywhere

CONTENTS

PREFACE, ix

ACKNOWLEDGMENTS, xiii

1

Dancing Under the Lash, 3

The Middle Passage, 3

The Plantation Environment, 13

Bals du Cordon Bleu, 48

2

Shoddy Confines: The Jook Continuum, 63

The Great Transition, 63

Jook Houses, Honky-Tonks, After-Hours Joints, 76

Rent Parties, Chittlin' Struts, Blue Monday Affairs, 94

3

Upper Shadies and Urban Politics, 121

Monday Night at the Paradise Ballroom, 121

Bells, Buzzers, an Air of Legitimacy, 135

Night Clubs, Show Bars, Cabaret Parties, 142

Dancin' in the Streets, 154

Black Elite Affairs, 162

CONTENTS

POSTSCRIPT, 173

NOTES, 177

INDEX, 213

PREFACE

THIS work examines one facet of African-American core culture: the dance arena. (For our purposes, a dance arena is any institution of social interaction in African-American life in which secular social dancing plays an integral part.) It investigates three questions: What are the primary institutions that allowed the development of dance among African-Americans? What sociohistorical circumstances influenced these institutions? What has been the significance of the dance?

The notion that dance has a significant place in the African-American cultural psyche and collective memory is not new; it serves as one of our operating assumptions. This study also assumes that blacks have used dance to articulate group experiences. All the dance institutions we examine, except for quadroon balls and formal elite balls, served the lower and working classes and developed in accordance with the work rhythms and social needs of their constituencies.

The bulk of the study offers an exploratory look at the dance arenas themselves, focusing primarily on Cleveland, Ohio, as a model of the postmigration urban environment. Lack of scholarly information led me to rely on participants who sponsored, patronized, or entertained in these dance arenas. Because of this dearth of information, I used a wide variety of sources, including newspapers, magazines, journals, novels, biographies, slave testimony, interviews, conversation, and manuscripts.

The study ranges in time from the introduction of English slavery in 1619 to the sociocultural explosions of the 1960s. This may seem an extended period, but from the perspective of evolving cultural institutions it is relatively short. Though its foundations reach centuries into the past, African-American dance is still very young; it acquired a national character only in the early nineteenth century. Although the study moves broadly from enslavement to the mid-twentieth century, the organization of the chapters is topical, not rigidly chronological. There is some discussion of slavery and a brief examination of dance on board slave vessels, but most of the book covers the postemancipation period. Despite some encouragement, I have not dealt with recent phenomena such as break dancing, house jams, or hip hop.

Once the investigation was underway, it became clear that black dance culture divided into two major categories. The first includes institutions that appear exclusively in the black community and essentially underground, and thus they required practically no assistance from public officials in order to function. This group, its roots embedded in the African past, includes the classic jook and its derivative forms, the after-hours joints, honky-tonks, and rent parties. I have collectively labeled them "the jook continuum." Like the illegal lottery known as "the numbers," the jook provided both entertainment and an economic alternative to people excluded from the mainstream economy.

The second category of dance arena required official cooperation in order to exist. I describe this group

as "the commercial urban complex." Examples include membership clubs, night clubs, dance halls, and
block parties. Primarily urban in character, these do
not exist in direct relationship with each other, as
does the first group, nor do they have direct historical
precursors in the African past.

As my research progressed, it became apparent
how much the political workings of a city helped
shape the cultural lives of its black citizens. Through
exercise of their authority, such as controlling licensing for dance halls and membership clubs, the white
establishment could influence black activity. White
cooperation in this area was forthcoming only when
whites saw some advantage in it for themselves. The
jook forms, on the other hand, remained primarily underground, away from the American cultural and political mainstream.

A persistent concern is the relationship of black
dance arenas to American society. Whites have stead-
ily borrowed from African-American dance—largely
without acknowledgment or appreciation of the source.
Indeed, the overall exclusion of blacks from mainstream American life remains a cultural fact. The elab-
oration of white supremacy into a system of
economic domination prevented African-Americans
from achieving either a higher level of economic
development or more complete cultural assimilation.
In spite of this, the African-American dance arena has
demonstrated a cultural resilience and recuperative
creativity.

The scholarly literature of African-American culture has largely ignored the central role of dance in
secular cultural institutions. At the same time, dance

studies (like Lynne Emery's *Black Dance* and Marshall and Jean Stearns's *Jazz Dance*) neglect institutions in which black social dance developed. The literature on popular entertainment occasionally credits African-Americans as contributors to entertainment trends, but by and large views black expression as exotic variations of corresponding white forms. Work on the American cabaret scene, such as Lewis Erenberg's *Steppin' Out,* as well as most work on jazz, neglects the role played by African-American dance arenas. Studies of black popular culture, such as David Toop's *The Rap Attack* or Steven Hager's *Hip Hop,* focus almost completely on recent phenomena. My hope is that examining the institutional contexts in which dance has flourished will enable us to better understand the lives of the people who created them.

ACKNOWLEDGMENTS

NO WORK, great or small, is the production of a solitary effort. I am indebted to numerous people in the production of this book. I owe special thanks to Arthur Paris, Robert Harris, The Rites and Reason Theatre of Brown University, George Bass, Rhett Jones, Wilson Moses, Icabod Flewellen, the Rockefeller Foundation in the Humanities, Robert F. Thompson, and John Szwed. I thank Ronald Jordan, who acted as my escort to numerous interviews in which my personal safety could not be guaranteed. I thank Lathan Donald, 129-116, an Ohio inmate serving several life sentences, who typed the initial manuscript. I thank my informants, who gave generously of their time and information. I acknowledge numerous friends who supported and encouraged my efforts. I feel especially indebted to Jimmy Gordon, my husband, who acted as my personal research librarian whenever I became stuck. And last, but certainly not least, thanks to the universal Creator, from whom I draw my strength.

JOOKIN'

DANCING UNDER THE LASH

To see an African dance is to witness his cultural past and present. . . . For the African, the fullest expression of art is dance.
—Lee Warren, *The Dance of Africa* (1972)

The Middle Passage

SOCIAL dancing links African-Americans to their African past more strongly than any other aspect of their culture. This is hardly surprising, because dance was (and is today) of central importance in West Africa. It is not only a routine communal activity, but an integral part of ceremonies that bind groups together as a people. It links one's personal identity to that of the group; events throughout the life cycle of the individual and the community are commemorated in dance: fattening house dances, fertility dances, and rite-of-passage dances.[1]

Dance also serves as a mediating force between people and the world of the gods. Specific dances and rhythms were appropriate for particular deities; commonly, a specific rhythm is assigned to every mask and every step that the dancers perform.[2] Indeed, dance is so much a part of the philosophy, customs, and sense of place that eliminating it would radically alter the African view of the universe.

Although dances unrelated to ritual exist today in West Africa, most traditional dances have been connected to or are performed during religious ceremonies. Since virtually all such ceremonies are public events, officials such as chiefs, elders, and priests must be able dancers. Those deficient in skill undergo several months of instruction before assuming office. We can say without exaggeration that dance competency, if not proficiency, is required of all individuals in traditional West African society.

The pervasive nature of West African dance inevitably drew it into the struggle between slavers and their captives. Capture and brutal treatment brought psychological and cultural transformation, but beyond that, European and American slavers hoped to destroy independent cultural expression among their new acquisitions. They attempted to appropriate dance and reshape it into an instrument of domination. This section is concerned with the slaves' ability to retain or transmute elements of their African cultures in their new environment.

Capture, branding, sale, and especially the dread "middle passage" across the Atlantic were unlike anything the captive Africans had previously experienced. The horror of the experience could only be increased by its unpredictability. Imagine the bewilderment of people herded together for a purpose and a destination they could only speculate about. Surrounded by a variety of African languages (Yoruba, Ibo, Wolof, Bambara, and Bakongo, to name a few) plus that of the slave master, individuals were isolated, wrenched from their communities and ancestors.

Once on board the slaver, the Africans were controlled by terror and intimidation and treated as cargo. Concerned about profits rather than humane treatment, traders were interested in keeping slaves alive and fit for sale. There were two philosophies for loading slave ships: the "tight pack" and the "loose pack." The tight-pack slavers consistently exceeded the legal number of slaves on their ships, subjecting the Africans to a long journey under unbelievably overcrowded conditions. The loose packers obeyed the legal limitations or crowded only slightly. Neither strategy was humane. The actual space allotment per slave under legal conditions was "that every man slave is to be allowed six feet by one foot four inches for room, every woman five feet ten by one foot four, every boy five feet by one foot two and every girl four feet six by one foot."[3] As a consequence of crowding and unsanitary conditions, slave mortality was high.

From the moment of capture, the slaves were under siege. The Europeans attempted to destroy their past and to crush their world view, particularly their religious beliefs, which held the keys to culture and personality. In the middle passage, captives were forbidden to practice their cultural or social rituals. From the beginning of the slave trade, captains and slave dealers debated how much African culture a slave should be allowed to retain. Some practices were condemned as immoral or uncivilized; others were forbidden for political reasons. The Europeans (later, Americans) recognized that controlling the slaves' culture helped ensure their subordination.

Traditional dance was, of course, forbidden on the slavers, but there is evidence that something called "dancing" occurred in the middle passage. What was it? It seems highly unlikely that a dance area as such existed on the deck of a slaving vessel. The writings of slave-ship captains are not explicit on the matter. Most captains mentioned dancing in a way that implies that slaves happily "danced" on the ships carrying them away from Africa, but some testimony points to purposefully deceptive language in these accounts. Thomas Clarkson, describing the intentions of witnesses called before Parliament to testify against a bill setting a limit on the number of slaves that could be transported per voyage, stated:

> It was the object of the witnesses, when examined, to prove two things; first, that regulations were unnecessary because the present mode of transportation was sufficiently convenient for the objects of it, as was well adopted to preserve their comfort and their health. They had sufficient room, sufficient air, and sufficient provisions. When upon deck, *they made merry and amused themselves with dancing*.[4] [emphasis in original]

Further on, Clarkson recounts the observations of less biased witnesses to this "dancing."

> Their [the slaves'] allowance consisted of one pint of water a day to each person; they were fed twice a day with yams and horse beans.
>
> After meals they jumped in their irons for exercise. This was so necessary for their health, that they were whipped if they refused to do it, and this

jumping has been termed dancing. On board most slave ships, the shackled slaves were forced to "dance" after meals.

The parts, says Mr. Claxton, . . . on which their shackles are fastened are often excoriated by the violent exercise they are thus forced to take, of which they made many grievous complaints to him. In his ship even those who had the flux, scurvy and such edematous swellings in their legs as made it painful to them to move at all were compelled to dance by the cat. [5]

"Dancing" was believed to have a healing effect on slaves, and was prescribed to prevent both scurvy and suicidal melancholy. According to George Howe, a medical student who sailed to the west coast of Africa in 1880, "In the barracoons it was known that if a negro was not amused and kept in motion he would mope, squat down with his chin on his knees and arms clasped about his legs and in a very short time die." On board this particular ship the remedy for diverting slaves from fatal melancholy was to give them rum and dance them: "The negroes seemed to tire of the monotony of things and some grog was daily distributed to the men and native songs and dances were constantly going on. The ingenuity of everyone was taxed to provide a new source of amusement." Similarly, Dr. Thomas Trotter, surgeon of the *Brookes* in 1783, reported, "After the morning meals came a joyless ceremony called 'dancing the slaves.' Those who were in irons were ordered to stand up and make what motions they could, leaving a passage for such as were out of irons to dance around the deck." [6]

"Dancing the slaves" was a regular activity, as evidenced by advertisements for musicians to work on slave ships. Usually several crew members paraded on deck with whips and cat-o-nine-tails, forcing the men slaves to jump in their irons, often until their ankles bled. One sailor explained to Parliament that he was employed to "dance" the men while another person "danced" the women. On ships with no designated musician, music was provided by a slave thumping on a broken drum, an upturned kettle, or an African banjo, or by a sailor with a fiddle, bagpipe, or other instrument. As they danced, some slaves sang, incorporating their experience into their music. One commentator sarcastically noted that the ship captains' descriptions of this "dancing" ignored the slaves' evident misery.

> We do all we can, insisted the captains, to promote the happiness of the slaves on board. They were brought up on deck for eight hours everyday, while their quarters were being cleaned out, and they were encouraged to dance—in chains. Encouraged, indeed, as other witnesses testified by the application of whips! Those with swollen or diseased limbs were not exempt from partaking of this joyous pastime, though the shackles often peeled the skin off their legs. The songs they sang of sorrow and sadness—simple ditties of their own wretched estate. [7]

Forced to sing as well as dance, slaves predictably chose somber songs. It is not known whether these were traditional or new songs. On some ships slaves were taught short songs to accompany their dances, and sometimes they were permitted to use instruments like tambourines that were brought aboard for them. Some were forced to improvise drums from materials at hand. Some slaves apparently resisted less than others, willing to adapt traditional music and dances to these new instruments. One ship's officer commented:

> Our blacks were a good-natured lot and jumped to the lash so promptly that there was not much occasion for scoring their naked flanks. We had tambourines aboard, which some of the younger darkies fought for regularly, and every evening we enjoyed the novelty of African war songs and ring dances, fore and aft, with the satisfaction of knowing that these pleasant exercises were keeping our stock in good condition and, of course, enhancing our prospects of making a profitable voyage.[8]

The slaves' point of view on such dancing is briefly expressed in a poem printed around 1790. "The Sorrows of Yamba; Or, the Negro Woman's Lamentation" presents the story of an African woman kidnapped from her village home and separated from her children, husband, and parents. The woman, Yamba, is sold to a cruel master and eventually converts to Christianity. The poem conveys the painful longing and sorrow that most slaves must have felt during these occasions.

> At the savage Captains beck;
> Now like Brutes they make us prance:
> Smack the Cat about the Deck,
> And in scorn they bid us dance.[9]

Slaves as groups or individuals were also forced to dance to entertain the captain or his guests. The guest of a Dutch slave trader described his host's mulatto slave girl: "When I dined with the Dutch general at the Mine, I saw her there, being brought in to dance before us, very fine, bearing the title of Madame Vanbukeline." In other instances, slaves inadvertently provided entertainment. In a narrative of a voyage to New Calabar River on the coast of Guinea, James Barbot, owner of the slave ship *Albion-Frigate,* which sailed in 1698 and 1699, describes the good care given to his slaves during the middle passage:

> It is true, we allow them much more liberty and use them with more tenderness than most other Europeans would think prudent, as we had them all on deck every day in good weather. . . . We took care they did wash from time to time, to prevent vermin which they are subject to. Towards evening, the blacks would divert themselves on the deck, as they thought fit; some conversing together, others dancing, singing or sporting after their manner, which often made us pastime, especially the females, who being apart from the males and on the quarter deck and many of them young sprightly maidens, full of jollity and good humor, afforded us an abundance of recreation. [10]

Some Europeans were not content with vicarious pleasure and participated in the slaves' dance. The surgeon aboard the Brazilian slave ship *Georgia* leaves us this account from 1827:

> On the first voyage out of Calabar we had not been out a week before I found that the captain and crew were desperadoes of the worst kind. Once off the coast the ship became half bedlam and half brothel. Ruiz, our captain, and his two mates set an example of reckless wickedness. They stripped them-

selves and danced with black wenches while our
crazy mulatto cook played the fiddle. There was little attempt at discipline and rum and lewdness
reigned supreme. [11]

As the surgeon endured six voyages with the *Georgia,*
he apparently found a way to remain aloof from these
activities.

Slave trading became such an industry that something approaching standard practices developed for
feeding, exercise, and containment of slaves. Techniques for "dancing" the slaves emerged as well, but
they were shaped by the continual threat of slave mutiny. Some cautious captains allowed only women and
children slaves to be unshackled while on deck; others
unshackled and danced slaves only after dark, when
the chance of mutiny seemed small.

Illegal slavers engaged in smuggling allowed slaves
little time on deck, and "dancing" had to be scheduled
with a watchful eye for patrol ships. Similarly, when
the international slave trade was outlawed in 1807,
methods for dancing the slaves were devised to guard
against possible capture by either police patrols or pirates. One technique was to bring only a portion of the
slaves on deck at a time. Capture by a patrol ship
meant heavy penalties: the crew was arrested and the
cargo confiscated. The slaves were either returned to
Africa or auctioned off in the New World. If capture
seemed imminent, captains avoided arrest by jetti-
soning the contraband. Sometimes the entire cargo,
slaves and food, was dumped into the ocean. [12]

So few Africans left written accounts of their experience that little is known about their participation
in the dancing. Harsh sanctions certainly discouraged

resistance, the rewards for exceptional dancing (such as an extra cup of water or trip to the slop buckets used as toilet facilities) might have encouraged participation. Liquor was sometimes used as an incentive for some dancers. Liquor and dance diverted the slaves' attention from their condition, and Europeans used them in combination. At the least, the opportunity to be on deck while dancing offered a brief period of relief from the hold.

We can only speculate about the degree to which the middle passage transformed dance for African slaves. Dance existed in a bizarre duality between the dancers and the slave traders. For most of the captive Africans, dance was a cultural vehicle used to mediate between mankind and the deities. African captives on slave vessels probably attempted to evoke deities who could assist them in revolt and escape. Indeed, they might have attributed their failures to their inability to perform ceremonies properly, with appropriate religious objects and the aid of the entire community. [13]

This forced dancing may also have been seen by the slaves as an opportune time to stage a mutiny or suicide. Creating noise and motion, slaves could distract at least a portion of the crew at one end of the ship. The elaborate precautions taken by ship captains indicate that slaves saw dancing as an opportunity to resist their enslavement. Slaves were watched constantly while on deck. [14] Slavers devised strategies to prevent mutiny or suicide, and to regain control in cases of rebellion. Some captains aimed ships' guns at the dancing slaves to intimidate them.

The pattern established on board the slave ship was reinforced in the plantation environment: dancing was done under the strict governance and supervision of whites who legitimized violence as a means of controlling the slave population. At the same time, resistance and dissembling became associated with dance aboard the slave ship. The African slaves learned to camouflage their hunger for freedom; an apparent accommodation to the circumstances of slavery became a survival mechanism. Once the slaves reached North America, they exploited dance as an opportunity to resist domination.

The Plantation Environment

Once safely through the middle passage and purchased, Africans were expected to adapt fairly quickly to bondage. Life under slavery, repressive though it was, allowed some opportunity for community and cultural development. It seems astonishing that any African customs could persist, but owners did not control all areas of slaves' lives. Unregulated sociocultural space provided Africans with some latitude in which aspects of African culture could survive.

At least two other factors help explain the survival of African-based traditions: first, some African cultural forms proved functional for the practitioners; second, they did not appear to threaten the slaveocracy. Once the African slaves left the ship and "settled in," they became part of the fabric of life in their new environment, with new acquaintances and group relationships. Shared customs cemented such relationships and unfamiliar ones provided material for new cultural amalgams. African groups were by no means undifferentiated, but they were culturally more similar to each other than any of them were to Europeans.

In the early days of the slave regime, the constant importation of new slaves served to shore up weakening cultural ties to Africa. Even after the international slave trade was outlawed, pirates and smugglers supplied a smaller number of Africans who probably renewed the vitality of African culture. The newly enslaved probably exerted a re-Africanization on plantation dance forms. [15]

The conditions of slavery in North America varied somewhat across time and region. Not all slaves lived on plantations. Some were house servants, urban laborers, or hands on small farms. On some plantations slaves worked in gangs or groups; on others they worked as individuals with task assignments. Work was the dominant feature of slave life, and the work pattern undoubtedly affected the model of culture that emerged. For example, the work song probably achieved a fuller development among slaves on work gangs than among those who worked alone. [16] The dancing among skilled urban artisans appears to have differed from that of field laborers. The type of work determined the slaves' daily routine and consequently their cultural materials. Thus the model of culture—determined by the work routines and the slaves' ethnic composition—varied from one region to the next. Just as one cannot speak of a national American culture early in the colonial period, African-American culture had not yet acquired its national character.

Whether they grew rice, tobacco, cane, or cotton, served in a household, or worked as an urban artisan, slaves had limited opportunity to establish independent culture. Whites, for example, attempted to eliminate slaves' access to drums. Such measures were less than entirely successful, but they created an environment that hindered slaves' attempts to assert their collective identity. Slaves managed to develop models of culture that retained their African character for more than three hundred years, but these models endured because whites did not immediately recognize them as threatening.

As the African was transformed into the African-American, several significant metamorphoses occurred. Most important for an understanding of black dance culture was a distinction between sacred and secular. For most Africans, the social and religious community were the same, and political leaders as well as human ancestors mediated between the living community and world of the deities. Unlike the western God, African ancestral deities embodied a wide range of seemingly contradictory attributes. The clear dichotomy of good and evil that marks Judeo-Christian religious figures was unknown to West Africans.

The major African deities (*orisha*) were capable of performing great feats—and great harm to humans. Like the Greek gods, but unlike the Christian, their nature was inherently erotic. They required appeasement and supplication in the form of ritualized sacrifices and offerings. North American Protestantism came to define African religious beliefs as sinful and strictly forbade their practice, but even among the African-Americans who converted to Christianity, African traditions remained vital. Equally important, much of African religious style, fervor, format, and predisposition in worship persisted in secular vestment.

Over time, a clear demarcation emerged between

sacred, ceremonial dance and the secular dancing associated with festivities and parties. The split began in the middle passage, and by the time the first generation of slaves was born on these shores the process was well underway.

Both sacred and secular dancing originated in an African worship system that included a wide range of praise methods, including a "party for the gods," or *bembe* as these religious parties came to be known in Cuba.[17] (The Cuban experience can illuminate some aspects of dance in the United States). At least three types of *bembe* were observed among the Lucumi (Cuban Yoruba): *bembe Lucumi, bembe Lucumi criollo,* and *suncho. Bembe Lucumi* was more generally African than the other two. Its songs were sung in the Yoruba language, its drum rhythms were strictly traditional and were executed on the sacred two-headed bata drum. *Bembe Lucumi criollo* permitted a loosening of tradition; its songs were in a creolized language and its rites were more communal and simpler. The third type, *suncho,* appears to have been the true "ocha party" or party for the gods. Unlike the other types of *bembe, suncho* did not always accompany a religious occasion. It appears to have been purely for enjoyment, with religion more pretext than a motive.[18] Although there is no evidence that the *bembe* ever established itself in North America, similar elements were probably retained in "the shouts" held both openly and surreptitiously among North American slaves. African religious elements—musical style, ecstatic behavior, spirit possession, and holy dancing—found expression in these shouts. Writer Frederick Law Olmsted leaves us this account:

On most of the large rice plantations which I have
seen in this vicinity, there is a small chapel, which
the Negroes use as their prayer house. The owner
of one of these told me that, having furnished the
prayer-house with seats having a back rail, his
Negroes petitioned him to remove it because it did
not leave them room enough to pray. It was explained to me that it is their custom, in social worship, to work themselves up to a great pitch of
excitement, in which they yell and cry aloud, and
finally shriek and leap up, clapping their hands and
dancing, as it is done at heathen festivals. The back
rail they found to seriously impede this exercise. [19]

Apparently American slaves did not confine their
African-based rituals and practices to purely religious
occasions. As one commentator noted:

Tonight I have been to a "shout" which seems to
me certainly the remains of some old idol worship.
The negroes sing a kind of chorus—three standing
apart to lead and clap—and then all the others go
shuffling round in a circle following one another
with not much regularity, turning round occasionally and bending the knees, and stamping so that
the whole floor swings. I never saw anything so
savage. They call it a religious ceremony, but it
seems more like a regular frolic to me. [20]

During numerous African religious ceremonies, particularly those of the Yoruba, music is performed by a
liturgical trio of sacred bata drums, namely, okonkolo,
itotele and iya. The "three standing apart to lead and
clap" mentioned here appear to be an adaptation of
this traditional West African pattern to a new sociocultural environment.

Though the ceremonial context and specific movements varied from group to group, the basic vocabulary of West African dance was strikingly similar across ethnic lines. As a result, interethnic assimilation in the new cultural environment was more easily facilitated in dance than in other aspects of the African culture, such as language.[21] Brought to the Americas in the motor-muscle memory of the various West African ethnic groups, the dance was characterized by segmentation and delineation of various body parts, including hips, torso, head, arms, hands, and legs; the use of multiple meter as polyrhythmic sensitivity; angularity; multiple centers of movement; asymmetry as balance; percussive performance; mimetic performance; improvisation; and derision. These esthetic and technical commonalities continued to be governing principles as dance moved from its sacred context to the numerous secular uses it acquired under slavery.

In North America institutions sometimes minimally supported the retention of African religious culture. Some slave masters established "praise houses" and permitted their slaves to "shout" or engage in secular dancing, even though their peers often disapproved. But the benefits often outweighed the disapproval, as one master testifies:

> I would build a house large enough, and use it for a
> dancehouse for the young, and those who wish to
> dance, as well as for prayer meetings, and for
> church on Sunday—making it a rule to be present
> myself occasionally at both, and my overseer al-
> ways. I know the rebuke in store about dancing, but
> I cannot help it. I believe negroes will be better dis-
> posed this way than any other.[22]

In general, however, slavery in the context of North American Protestantism proved more hostile to African customs than slavery under Catholic auspices. French and Spanish Catholics introduced their slaves to a pantheon of saints that the Africans came to associate with their own deities and so with their traditional religious practices. Thus, the African theological background to many of these practices (including dance) might disappear while the practice itself or a version of it survived, eventually relegated by the practitioners to the realm of the secular, magic, or folk custom. African-American dance, hoodoo, and folk medicine are clear examples. And as we shall see, a similar process occurred on a broader institutional level.

Slaves performed a wide variety of dances, including a few adopted from their masters, but the majority were distinctly African in character. Among the dances they created were wringin' and twistin' (which would later form the basis of the twist), the buzzard lope, breakdown, pigeon wing, cakewalk, Charleston, "set de flo'," snake hips (the basis for all later African-American dances requiring sharp-popping accents demarcating each line of movement as in the jerk and the breaking style known as "pop locking"), and the shout, which unlike the others retained both a sacred and secular character. Many of the dances consisted of a basic step and a series of improvisational embellishments, which usually initially imitated motions of the work routine. Former slaves frequently mentioned "pitchin' hay," "corn shuckin'," and "cuttin' wheat" as embellishments in the cakewalk.[23] In this regard too the slaves were relying on African traditions in creating new dances; a large number of African dances celebrated through imitation significant environmental factors such as herd size, events in the life cycle, or physical labor and work routines.

The amalgamation of traditional African dance principles and the slaves' responses to their New World experience can be seen in the dance known as "set de flo'." Set de flo' took a variety of forms, but in the most interesting a circle was drawn to make an area in which the competing dancers performed. The musician, usually a fiddler, would call out complicated step routines for the dancers to negotiate without stepping on or outside the drawn circle. Dancers often demonstrated their dexterity by placing a glass of water on their heads, performing as many steps as possible without spilling the water.

The challenge posed by the fiddler-caller, familiar to West Africans, calls upon the dancer to perform difficult combinations of steps. The best performers are those who can meet the challenge while maintaining control and coolness. In the African esthetic, balance is achieved through the combination of opposites. Although dancers may be performing a fury of complex steps or figures, they must never lose equilibrium or control. This principle of asymmetry as balance can be observed among many West African groups. Shango, or thundergod devotees, sometimes dance with a container of burning fire balanced on their heads. Among the Egbado Yoruba people, gifted dancers with delicate terra cotta sculptures on their heads demonstrate raw energy in the movements of arms and torso.[24] This principle was later demonstrated in the foot-flashing repetitions of tap dancers like Jimmy Mordacai as well as in break dancing.

Unfortunately, little is known of the secret and well-hidden dances of slaves, but their observed activities indicate that they did not substantially modify the African dance vocabulary or all of the meaning, particularly the qualities of derision and resistance.

The outlawing of the international slave trade in 1807 increased the difficulty of importing Africans to the Americas; after the mid-nineteenth century, most blacks in North American had been born there. This change affected the development of African-American culture in two ways. First, it meant that each new generation would be further removed from contact with indigenous Africans or African cultural practices. Second, blacks in North America, unlike those in the West Indies or parts of Latin America, were not numerous enough to sustain specific ethnic traditions in their cultural complex. Thus, the conditions in North America encouraged the interethnic blending of African customs. Particular traits and habits were subsumed or absorbed, while sustaining something of their original character, and became the initial outline for an emerging African-American cultural complex.

Equally important in the emergence of an African-American culture was the increasing use of the cotton gin. The enormous growth in cotton production early in the nineteenth century gave the South a more homogeneous work culture than it had previously known. "King Cotton" blanketed areas that had primarily grown tobacco, rice, or indigo. Cultural historians have yet to examine the ways in which the new dominance of cotton synchronized work rhythms across regions that had differed significantly. It affected language, daily routines, and yearly schedules.

It changed the environment and modified the tools as well as the materials from which the folk culture was created. From Virginia through Texas, slaves had the new experience of a universal force acting on their cultural lives. While southern culture was never homogenous, it was overwhelmingly dominated by the cotton plantation. The plantation system generally and the demands of individual masters affected the development of African-American culture.

On the plantation, slaves danced for themselves as celebration, recreation, and mourning as well as for their masters' entertainment. As in the middle passage, dancers were sometimes rewarded with money, extra food, or a pass to another plantation. Yet slaveholders were well aware that dance could function as a form of social intercourse, cultural expression, assimilation mechanism, and political expression. Because it was a means of solidifying the slave community, dance could threaten white dominance. Indeed, slaves used dance to camouflage insurrectionary activity. Masters who permitted slave dancing did so with care, and did so hoping to pacify the slaves' desire to rebel.

Still, most masters recognized the usefulness of allowing at least some dancing among their slaves. Almost all slaves were allowed to celebrate Christmas, and some form of dancing was usually part of the celebration.[25] An article in a southern journal describes the holidays on one plantation:

> Holidays—We usually have two, one about the 4th
> of July and one at Christmas. The one in July is
> celebrated with a dinner and whiskey. The
> Christmas holiday is a very different thing. It lasts

from four to six days and during the *jubilee* it is difficult to say who is master. The servants are allowed the largest liberty. They are furnished with whiskey and egg-nog freely, and all the means necessary for good dinners and suppers. They are permitted to invite their friends from neighboring plantations, and to enjoy themselves in any way that suits them. Dancing is their favorite amusement and they go to it, I can assure you with a "perfect rush."[26]

Christmas festivities commonly included dancing, drinking, extra food, and visits to other plantations. One former slave recalled that on Christmas her parents could see each other: "Well, Marse Harriston didn't 'low paw to see may 'cep twice a year—laying-by time and Christmas." Another describes the festivities and the passes that limited slaves' mobility:

Roun' Christmas we git three days holiday as theah's plenty uh dances and shoutin then. We goes tuh the ownuh and gits a ticket an we all gathuhs at the same place an we shouts an kick up with each othuh, but wen yuh ticket out, ef yuh dohn come back, the patrol will git yuh and then yuh gits whipped.[27]

John Pierpont, minister and journalist, recorded his impressions of Christmas on Colonel Alston's Monjetta plantation in South Carolina in 1805, paying special attention to the contrast between the slaves' Christmas privileges and their usual privations.

Throughout the state of South Carolina, Christmas is a holiday together with 2 of the succeeding days, for all literary seminaries, but more especially for the Negroes. On these days the chains of slavery with which the blacks are loaded and in which they toil unceasingly for their masters, are loosed. A smile is seen on every countenance, and the miseries of the year seem amply recompensed by this season of hilarity and festivity.

No restraint is imposed upon their inclinations, no one calls their attention from the enjoyment of all those delights which the most unconstrained freedom proffers. Children visit their parents; husbands their wives; brothers and sisters each other, who live at a distance and partake the pleasures of social connexions of which they are deprived during the remaining part of the year.

On the morning of Christmas, Col. Alston gave orders that as many beeves might be butchered as to supply all with meat, which as a general thing is not allowed them. No less than 21 bullocks fell sacrifices to the festivity. On my first waking, the sound of the serenading violin and drum saluted my ears even in retirement. During almost the whole of the second and 3 afternoons, the portico was crowded with these dancers, who by their countenance reminded me of the ancient nymphs, satyrs and fauns, and the fiddlers and dancers brought Pan and Timotheus freshly to mind. Some of them who were native Africans did not join the dance with the others but, by themselves gave us a specimen of the sports and amusements with which the benighted and uncivilized children of nature, divest themselves, before they became acquainted with the more refined and civilized amusements of life. Clapping their hands was their music and distorting their frames into the most unnatural figures and emitting the most hideous noises is their dancing. [28]

Whether the celebration was elaborate or small, the Christmas holidays involved some break from the normal routine and some generosity toward slaves. One former slave was treated to Christmas day off and "a big dinner wid all kinds good things to eat spread out in de yard"; Adeline Johnson remembered Christmas as a time of virtual freedom: slaves on her master's plantation were given a week off and some were allowed to travel to neighboring plantations without a pass. [29]

With so much going on, masters were hard pressed to keep track of slave activity for three days, sometimes more. Some masters shared the monitoring responsibilities by staggering the dances and parties so that slaves on one plantation could entertain slaves from neighboring plantations and in turn be entertained. [30] But such cooperation was by no means common; in fact, some masters forbade their slaves to leave the plantation during the period of generalized celebration.

> Believing that the strolling about of Negroes for a week at a time, during what are called Christmas Holidays, is productive of much evil, the writer has set his face against the custom. Christmas is observed as a sacred festival. On that day as good a dinner as the plantation will afford is served for the Negroes, and they all sit down to a common table, but the next day we go to work. From considerations both of morality and needful rest and recreation to the negro, I much prefer a week in July, when the crop is laid by, to giving three days at Christmas. [31]

During the Christmas season slave dances were less restricted, generally lasting longer than ordinary dances, and they were frequently combined with other celebrations, such as weddings. These festivities might go on all day and into the next morning.[32] During the holiday, the slaves shed their work clothes and dressed in their best.

While almost any holiday celebrated by the masters—Easter, Fourth of July, Whitsuntide—might also be celebrated by their slaves, Christmas appears to have been the most elaborate festivity of the year and probably for that reason the most favored by slaves. As an eagerly anticipated event, Christmas became the ultimate reward for good behavior, and masters often threatened to abridge the holiday as they disciplined slaves.[33]

On many plantations, at least part of Saturday and usually all day Sunday were a break from regular work routines. Masters made Saturday afternoons a time for slaves to attend to their personal needs such as washing, gardening, or cleaning up the quarters. In many instances, slaves were assigned tasks for Saturday, so few considered the time their own. One farmer stated: "I give all my females half of every Saturday to wash and clean up, my cook washing for young men and boys through the week." On most plantations all hands stopped work on Saturday at noon. Practices varied, however, and were subject to seasonal changes and regional differences. Robert Collins, a Georgia planter, describes his policy on Saturday labor:

> *Hours of Work*—In the winter time and in the sickly season of the year, all hands should have breakfast before leaving the house. This they can do and get to work by sunrise, and stop no more until twelve o'clock; then rest one hour for dinner then work

until night. In the spring and summer they should
go at light, and stop at 8 o'clock for breakfast then
work until 12 o'clock and two hours for dinner, and
work from 2 o'clock and 'till night. All Hands stop
on Saturday at 12 o'clock and take the afternoon for
cleaning up their houses and clothes, so as to make
a neat appearance on Sunday morning. [34]

Generally masters encouraged and provided for
regular weekly dances, keenly aware that they helped
maintain morale. One small farmer leaves us this account on the management of Negroes:

Negroes are gregarious; they dread solitariness, and
to be deprived from the little weekly dances and
chit-chat. They will work to death rather than be
shut-up. I know the advantage though I have no
jail, my house being a similar one, yet used for other purposes.
    I have a fiddle in my quarters and though some
of my good brethren in the church would think
hard of me, yet I allow dancing; ay I buy the fiddle
and encourage it, by giving the boys occasionally a
big supper. [35]

Some masters even purchased slave musicians to provide music. A Mississippi planter felt some pride in his
efforts to arrange a good dance:

I must not omit to mention that I have a good fiddler, and keep him well supplied with catgut, and I
make it his duty to play for the negroes every Saturday night until 12 o'clock. They are exceedingly
punctual in their attendance at the hall, while
Charley's fiddle is always accompanied with Ihurod
on the triangle, and Sam to "pat."[36]

Most secular dances occurred primarily in conjunction with a special observance, such as a holiday or weekend. With the ability to curtail or encourage slave dance culture, masters sought to turn occasions to their own use. When slaves made their own dances —and they often did—they accepted a terrible risk of harsh punishment. Slave owners regarded even such frolicsome activities as collective disobedience that seriously threatened their control. They were not wrong.

Slaves accepted dances and other celebrations as a relief from the burdens of their hard lives, relishing every form of enjoyment permitted them, including food, drinking, fellowship with other slaves, and, of course, dancing. And slaves broke the rules. Though drinking except when approved by owners was forbidden, slaves enjoyed homemade alcoholic beverages at these frolics, and they distributed them clandestinely when necessary. Apparently some slaves even built their own stills. John Crawford, born into slavery in Mississippi around 1837, leaves us this account of his grandfather's still:

> Grandpappy used to own a still which was run by grandpappy's friend Billy Buck, an old nigger. They made whisky out of corn and made whisky out of peaches. Then they made apple cider and grape wine and dandelion wine and alder (eldeberry) wine. The alder was for the niggers. At the parties and at Christmas the niggers got plenty of whisky.[37]

In William B. Smith's account of a dance he witnessed in the lower end of Prince Edward, Virginia, the slaves of Mr. Samuel Poe had brewed a barrel of persimmon beer and obtained permission from their master to have what they called a "beer dance."

Here the banjor-man, was seated on the beer barrel, in an old chair. *Tumming* his banjor, grinning with ludicrous gesticulations and playing off his wild notes to the company. Before him stood two athletic blacks, clapping *Juber* to the notes of the banjor; the fourth black man held in his right hand a jug gourd of persimmon beer, and in his left, a dipper or water-gourd, to serve the company while two black women were employed in filling the fireplace, six feet square, with larded persimmon dough. The rest of the company, male and female were dancers. The clappers rested the right foot on the heel, and its clap on the floor was in perfect unison with the notes of the banjor and palms of the hands on the corresponding extremities. The dancers having the most ludricuous twists, wry jerks, and flexile contortions of the body and limbs, that human imagination can divine. [38]

The musical instruments at American slave dances were primarily African in nature and strongly resembled instruments found in other New World slave communities. And although slave musicians did adopt certain European instruments such as the violin, the fiddle so frequently mentioned in descriptions of early slave dances was not the European violin but rather an African gourd fiddle that, like the banjo, was constructed by slaves from a technique passed down from older Africans. Isaac D. Williams, a former slave, recalls:

We generally made our own banjos and fiddles, and I had a fiddle that was manufactured out of a gourd, with horse hair strings and a bow made out of the same material. When we made a banjo we would first of all catch what we called a ground hog, known in the north as a woodchuck. After tanning his hide, it would be stretched over a piece of timber fashioned like a cheese box, and you couldn't tell the difference in sound between that homely affair and a handsome store bought one.[39]

Mack Chaney, a Mississippi ex-slave, tells of his father, a full-blooded African and skilled musician:

He made himself a fiddle outa pine bark and usta play fer us to dance. He taught me to dance when I wuz little like dey did in Africa. Day dance by deselves or swing each other 'round. Dey didn't know nothing 'bout dese "huggin" dances. I'd be settin on my daddy's lap and he'd tell me all 'bout when he lived in Africa. He usta play de' fiddle and sing 'bout Africa—Dat Good Ole Land.[40]

Throughout West Africa today people play the prototype of the gourd fiddle, or susa, as it is known among the Fulani people. According to Mandingo griot Foday Musa Suso the susa is an ancient instrument.[41] A gourd forms the body, and horsehair the strings; the bow is bamboo with horsehair. The gourd fiddle is played while held in the bend of the elbow rather than under the chin.

In addition to banjos and fiddles, drums, tambourines, gourds, bones, quills, kettles, hand claps, jawbones, hoes, wooden boxes, and any metal pot or piece accompanied dancing on the plantation. Although some sources state that these instruments were adopted primarily as a substitute for the outlawed drum, all have been widely used in places where drum playing is common, such as Cuba and Brazil, and apparently were taken up for their own sake or retained from Africa.

Wash Wilson, born a slave in Louisiana and taken to Texas before the Civil War, described the types of musical instruments used at slave dances; the variety of objects and techniques testifies to the ingenuity of slave musicians.

> Us take pieces of sheep's rib or cow's jaw or a piece iron, with a old kettle, or a hollow gourd and some horsehair to make de drum. Sometimes dey'd get a piece of tree trunk and hollow it out and stretch a goat's or sheep's skin over it for de drum. Dey'd be one to four foot high and a foot up to six foot 'cross. In gen'ral two niggers play with de fingers or sticks on dis drum. Never seed so many in Texas, but dey made some. Dey'd take de buffalo horn and scrape it out to make de flute. Dat sho' be heard a long ways off. Then dey'd take a mule's jaw-bone and rattle de sticks 'cross its teeth. Then day'd take a barrel, and stretch a ox's hide cross one end and a man sat 'stride de barrel, and beat on dat hide with he hands and he feet and iffen he get to feelin' de music in his bones, he'd beat on dat barrel with his head. 'Nother man beat on wooden sides with sticks. [42]

Frederick Douglass remarked that slave "holidays were among the most effective means in the hands of slaveholders of keeping down the spirit of insurrection among slaves . . . but for those [dances, frolics, holidays] the rigors of bondage would have become too severe for endurance and the slave would have been forced to a dangerous desperation."[43] Many slaveholders certainly saw it that way. Yet no matter how much these occasions were intended to encourage resignation, slaves were able to seize dances as opportunities to resist white domination. A considerable

amount of insurrectionary activity took place during
slave holidays and days off, and even in tightly controlled situations themes of resistance were evident in
both urban and rural settings. Slaves and masters
were continually engaged in a struggle for control. Resistance met with new forms of repression, which in
turn bred more resistance.

Fear of slave rebellions, especially as the need
for labor intensified, called for extreme measures. In
South Carolina, for example, the demand for slaves increased as rice cultivation replaced animal husbandry.
After 1698, South Carolina imported Africans in such
numbers that the black population outnumbered
whites.[44] Numerous slave insurrections resulted in
legislation aimed to prevent slaves from visiting other
plantations; from using drums, horns, or any other instrument that might signal rebellion; from having
gatherings of more than a few people; or having gatherings without a specified proportion of armed white
men present. In Charleston, a piece of legislation enacted in 1740, the year following the Stono Rebellion,
was specifically aimed at occasions on which slaves
might gather for dances. Section 36 is worth quoting
in its entirety:

> And for that as it is absolutely necessary to the
> safety of this province that all due care be taken to
> restrain the wanderings and meetings of negroes
> and other slaves, at all times, and more especially
> on Saturday nights, Sundays and other holidays,
> and their using and carrying wooden swords, and
> other mischievous and dangerous weapons, or use
> or keeping of drums, horns, or other loud instru-
> ments, which may call together or give sign or no-

tice to one another of their wicked designs and purpose; and that all masters, overseers and others
may be enjoined, diligently and carefully to prevent
the same, *Be it enacted* by the authority aforesaid,
That it shall be lawful for all masters, overseers and
other persons whomsoever, to apprehend and take
up any negro other slave that shall be found out of
the plantation of his or their master or owner, at
any time Especially on Saturday nights, Sundays or
other holidays, not being on lawful business, and
with a letter from their master, or a ticket, or not
having a white person with them; and the said
negro or other slave or slaves, met or found out of
the plantation of his or their master or mistress,
though with a letter or ticket, if he or they be armed
with such offensive weapons aforesaid, him or them
to disarm, take up whip: And whatsoever master,
owner, or overseer shall permit or suffer his or their
negro or other slave or slaves, at any time hereafter,
to beat drums, blow horns, or use any other loud
instruments, or whosoever shall suffer and countenance any public meeting or feasting of strange
negroes, or slaves in their plantations, shall forfeit
ten pounds, current money, for every such offense,
upon conviction or proof as aforesaid; *provided,* an
information or other suit be commenced within one
month after forfeiture thereof for the same.[45]

Laws forbidding the use of drums changed the nature
of events where dancing occurred among African
slaves and eventually affected the profile of black culture in North America.

Because they brought together large groups of
blacks, slave dancing affairs provided opportunities
to exchange information and plot insurrections; when

slaves outnumbered whites, spontaneous eruptions of violence were possible. Indeed, ample evidence indicates that slave insurrections were either plotted at dances or scheduled to take place on occasions that involved dancing. One analysis revealed that 35 percent of rebellions in the British Caribbean were either planned for or took place in late December.[46] The high pitch of emotions at these dances could serve as a pretext for touching off a previously planned revolt.[47] The links between dance and rebellion give these occasions a striking resemblance to war dances, or dances in which preparation for battle was the central theme. An armed rebellion in South Carolina in 1730 was planned to begin when slaves "should assemble in the neighborhood of the town, under the pretense of a dancing bout." Similarly, an account of the Stono Rebellion in South Carolina in 1739 reports that slaves seized weapons and killed a number of whites; marching southwestward with "drums beating and colors flying," they were joined by others. After marching about twelve miles, they "halted in an open field, and began to sing and dance, by way of triumph. During these rejoicings, the militia discovered them, and stationed themselves in different places around them to prevent them from making their escape."[48]

Throughout slave territory the drum had long been used to signal public gatherings and dances, and its use continued even after being forbidden. Perhaps some slaves who joined the Stono uprising initially thought that they were being called to a dance: "They increased every minute by new Negroes coming to them, so that they were about Sixty, some say a hundred, on which they halted in a field and set to

dancing, Singing and beating Drums, to draw more
Negroes to them."[49]

Religious meetings and field work also gave slaves
opportunity to plan and execute rebellions, and virtually every gathering of slaves was viewed with suspicion. Social gatherings of one sort or another, which
occurred continually, induced a high level of paranoia
among whites, but both whites and blacks came to regard dances as especially dangerous.[50]

Plantation affairs, whether held on a holiday or a
weekend, were essential in the development of regional culture. But in the areas immediately on the edges
of towns such as Charleston, New Orleans, or Mobile,
large public dances held by urban slaves had a different
character. Urban slaves were regarded by many plantation owners as lacking regulation and restraint. For
the most part they lived away from the watchful eye of
their master. Most free blacks and skilled artisans re-
sided in urban areas; and since slaves who could hire
out their labor and rent their own shelter were virtually indistinguishable from free blacks, they enjoyed
more autonomy than plantation slaves.[51]

Law forbade slaves to be on the street at night without a pass from their masters; however, it was impos-
sible to detect every instance of violation. The relative
liberty of movement among urban slaves was a continuing source of complaint from white urban residents.[52] Plantation owners, fearing their slaves would
be drawn to a life of greater liberty, discouraged association with urban slaves.

At plantation dances, the overseer or the master
could control access to his property. Dances held on
public property, however, defeated such strictures.

These large public affairs, like organized worship services for slaves, provided an arena in which black culture could flourish irrespective of status. They brought together plantation laborer, house servant, urban artisan, and free Negro in a celebration of African-based dance. Urban slaves sometimes took the liberty of holding a dance without approval or the required supervision of armed whites; these affairs could attract 200 slaves or more, and crowd control was difficult. The *South Carolina Gazette* described one such unsanctioned affair:

> The Stranger had once an opportunity of seeing a Country Dance, Rout or Cabal of Negroes, within 5 miles distance of this town, on a Saturday night; and it may not be improper here to give a description or that assembly. It consisted of about 60 people, 5-6th from Town, every one of whom carried something, in the manner just described; as bottled liquors of all sorts, Rum, Tongues, Hams, Beef, Geese, Turkies and Fowls both drest and raw, with many luxuries of the table as sweetmeats, pickles & (which some did not scruple to acknowledge they obtained by means of false keys, procured from a Negro in Town, who could make any Key whenever the impression of the true one was brought to him in wax) without doubt, were stolen and brought thither, in order to be used on the present occasion or to be concealed and disposed of by such of the gang as might have the best opportunities for this purpose: *Moreover,* they were provided with Music, Cards, Dice &c. . . .
>
> Then they *danced, betted, gamed, swore, quarreled, fought,* and did everything that the *most modern* accomplished gentlemen are *not ashamed of.*

The atmosphere of frolic and confusion provided opportunities for contacts among insurrectionists, runaways, and other dissenters. The *South Carolina Gazette* continues:

> They also had their private committees; whole deliberations were carried on in too low voice, and with much caution, as not to be overheard by the others much less by the Stranger, who was concealed in a deserted adjacent hut, where the humanity of a well disposed grey headed Negro man had placed him, pitying his *seeming* indigence and distress. The members of this secret council had much the appearance of Doctors in deep and solemn consultation upon life or *death* which indeed might have been the scope of their meditations at the time. No less than 12 fugitive slaves joined this respectable company before midnight, 3 of whom were mounted on good horses; these after delivering a good quality of Mutton, Lamb and Veal, which they brought with them, directly associated with one or other of the private consultations; and went off about an hour before day beging supplied with liquor &c and perhaps also received some instructions.[53]

Any dance format provided the potential for resistance; however, urban public dances, which occurred outdoors, provided the best opportunities for planned insurrection. Antoine Simon Le Page du Pratz, a Louisiana resident from 1718 to 1734, observed:

> Nothing is more to be dreaded than to see the Negroes assemble together on Sundays, since under pretence of Calinda, or the dance, they sometimes get together to the number of three or four

hundred, and make a kind of Sabbath, which it is always prudent to avoid; for it is in those tumultuous meetings that they sell what they have stolen to one another, and commit many crimes. In these likewise they plot their rebellions.[54]

Assemblies of this sort were apparently common in Louisiana, particularly in and around New Orleans. Slaves would gather in several locations around the city on Saturday and Sundays to sing, drum, and dance until dark. By 1786, however, the law forbade slaves to dance on public squares on Sundays and holy days until after evening church service. A visitor to the city in 1799 reports that after dinner on Sunday he saw "vast numbers of negro slaves, men, women, and children, assembled together on the levee, dancing in large rings." In 1804, a Louisiana observer, John Watson reported seeing dancing Negroes "in great masses on the levee on Sundays." Four years later another observer in New Orleans witnessed "twenty different dancing groups of the wretched Africans collected together to perform their *worship* after the manner of their country. They have their own national music, consisting for the most part of a long kind of narrow drum of various sizes from two to eight feet in length, three or four of which make a band." By 1817, dancing in New Orleans proved troublesome enough for the city to restrict it to Sundays before sundown and to one location, Congo Square. In this sense, the establishment of Congo Square, though it led to an inter-African mixing, contained rather than encouraged slave dancing and culture.[55]

New Orleans and Charleston were by no means the only locations for public slave dances and celebrations. In Somerset County, Maryland, complaints were lodged with the judicial authority that slaves were "drunke on the Lords Day beating their Negro drums by which they call considerable Number of Negroes together in some Certaine places." Similar complaints in early nineteenth-century St. Louis brought out the military to "suppress riots" among free and enslaved blacks gathered at public dances.[56]

Throughout North Carolina, particularly in the areas surrounding Wilmington, Fayetteville, Hilton, Edenton, New Bern, and Hillsboro, slaves danced publicly and celebrated the John Canoe festival. Author Harriet Brent Jacobs describes the tradition:

> Every child rises early on Christmas morning to see the Johnkannaus. Without them, Christmas would be shorn of its greatest attraction. They consist of companies of slaves from the plantations, generally of the lower class. Two athletic men, in calico wrappers, have a net thrown over them, covered with all manner of bright-colored stripes. Cows tails are fastened to their backs, and their heads are decorated with horns. A box, covered with sheepskin is called the gumbo box. A dozen beat on this, while others strike triangles and jawbones, to which bands of dancers keep time. For a month previous they are composing songs, which are sung on this occasion. These companies, of a hundred each, turn out early in the morning, and are allowed to go around 'till twelve o'clock, begging for contributions. Not a door is left unvisited where there is the least chance of obtaining a penny or a glass of rum. They do not drink while they are out, but carry the rum home in jugs, to have a carousal. These Christmas donations frequently amount to

twenty or thirty dollars. It is seldom that any white
man or child refused to give them a trifle. If he
does, they regale his ears with the following song

> Poor massa, so dey say;
> Down in de heel, so dey say;
> Got no money, so dey say;
> Not one shillin, so dey say:
> Got A mighty bless you, so dey say.[57]

The climax of the John Canoe doorstep entreaty
came when the company broke into the buzzard lope,
a dance well known to African-Americans in the coast-
al Carolinas. Anthropologist Melville Herskovits is
probably correct in speculating that the Yankoro or
buzzard of the Ashanti people is the likely origin of this
festival name. Certainly these performances in the
Carolinas were remarkably similar to John Canoe festivals held throughout the West Indies and even with
the Dia de Reyes celebrations in Cuba.[58]

Another annual event was the Pinkster celebration, familiar to the Dutch and Africans in Dutch-
settled areas, particularly New York. Usually beginning on the first Monday of Pentecost, this celebration
involved weeks of preparation and lasted from three to
seven days and coincided with the Dutch observance
of Pentecost.

When the long-awaited opening day arrived, slaves
from the countryside made their way to the nearest
town or city—New York City, Kingston, Albany,
Poughkeepsie, to name but a few—to join with the
urban colored in the carnival. The Albany festivities
topped all others. There the celebration was held at
the head of State Street, later the site of the State
Capitol. Booths were set up to dispense refresh-

ments of all sorts, including liquor, for the ban on strong drinks was temporarily lifted. A master of ceremonies presided, his principal task being to beat on the kettle-drum which provided the music for the singing, dancing, and parading which enlivened the occasion. In New York City dancing contests between local and Long Island slaves were staged in the streets for the entertainment of all, as well as for whatever shillings might be tossed to the contestants. The "jug" and the more difficult "breakdown" were performed to the rhythm of clapping hands and stamping feet.[59]

Like the John Canoe festivals in North Carolina and Jamaica (and like King Zulu in contemporary Mardi Gras), Pinkster festivities centered on a "king." Two historical accounts refer to an African who served as king for many years. One spoke of "'Charley of the Pinkster Hill' who was brought from Angola, in the Guinea Gulf, in his infant days, and purchased by a rich merchant living on the eastern bank of the Hudson. 'King Charles' was said to have royal blood in his veins." The second Pinkster account describes its "king" as a "colored harlequin":

Dressed in a coat of the military, decked out with colored ribbons, his legs bare and a little black hat with a pompom on one side, he was seated on a hollow log, which had each end covered with skins and served as a drum for dancing. Other negroes had eel pots covered with skin which they beat with their hands while they sang a song that had a refrain "Hi-a bomba bomba" which it was said was brought over from Africa. To this music the negroes danced. There were also gingerbread booths and side shows, and under the charge of the elderly

women all the young gentry were taken out to see
the sights.[60]

Throughout New England—in Norwich, Hartford,
Derby, and New Haven, Connecticut; in Newport and
Kingston, Rhode Island; Salem, Massachusetts, and
Portsmouth, New Hampshire—large annual celebrations known as "election day" were celebrated. The
festivities included a parade, dining, and dancing as
well as an election of a "Negro governor."

> These days of relaxation were made the occasion
> for a pompous and ceremonious parade by the
> negroes. They decked themselves out in striking or
> fantastic costumes, and on horseback or on foot ac-
> companied their "governor" through the streets.
> The parade included an accompaniment of hideous
> music, and was followed by a dinner and dance in
> some commodious hall hired for the purpose.
> Sometimes, however, the dinner and dance were
> not preceded by the parade. The central figure in
> these functions was the "governor," who was a *per-
> son of commanding importance.*[61]

The earliest known "Negro election day" is believed to have occurred in Salem, Massachusetts,
on May 27, 1741. Probably the last "Negro governor"
was elected in Humphreysville, Connecticut, in
1856.[62] "Election day" and the other festivals in
which a "king" or "governor" was chosen parallel black
Latin American and West Indian celebrations and
seem to derive from African political institutions.

> In their own land they had elected kings or chiefs
> chosen from among descendants of royal blood, and
> many practices of a judicial and social nature which
> bear a strong resemblance to those found among

them in America. As time went on these customs were greatly modified, partly by association with different customs, but chiefly through the mere action of time and the failure of fresh arrivals from Africa, until finally the meetings became little more than an opportunity for a good time. [63]

As we have seen, urban slaves and free blacks enjoyed fairly unrestricted access to public spaces. In contrast, plantation slaves occupied a narrower sphere. Social visits and celebrations were limited by the demands of agricultural work and cautious masters. Even masters who encouraged gatherings scheduled them as a reward for particularly arduous work—after a harvest, for example—or perhaps before, as an inducement.

Corn shucking or corn husking was a fairly common group activity on plantations. It required long hours of labor in addition to the normal day's work routine, and drew together all plantation slaves—household and agricultural workers, plus all the children. Competition between shucking teams, which gave the slaves a feeling of control over their work, made it tolerable. An ex-slave from Georgia recalled:

> In corn shucking time no padderolers would ever bother you. We would have a big time at corn shuckings. They would call up the crowd and line the men up and give them a drink. I was a corn general—would stand out high above everybody, giving out corn songs and throwing down corn to them. There would be two sides of them, one side trying to outshuck the other. [64]

Meager prizes for the winning side were generally not enough to make the occasion festive, but its social nature enabled some slaves to remember corn shuckings with fondness. A *New York Sun* article describes the lively atmosphere surrounding the corn shucking: "The corn was divided into two piles as big as a house and two captains were appointed. Each chose sides just as the captains in spelling matches do, and then the fun began."[65]

Outside of the routine organization of plantation life, corn shuckings represented an opportunity for slaves to gather as a community. They momentarily masked the divisions of work status, caste, and class, and provided an environment in which slave culture could develop. The need for additional labor sometimes brought slaves from neighboring plantations (I have found no evidence that urban slaves augmented the work force at shuckings). Community relations were established, revised, and re-created at the corn shuckings, giving rise to community standards and crystallizing local culture.

In time corn shuckings developed into a richly textured form that featured dance as well as songs in the call-and-response pattern. David C. Barrow, Jr., observed a dance that accompanied a corn shucking:

> With the cotillion a new and very important office,
> that of "callerout," though of less importance
> than the fiddler, is second to no other. He not only
> calls out the figures, but explains them at length
> to the ignorant, sometimes accompanying them
> through the performance. He is never at a loss,
> "genmen to de right" being a sufficient refuge in
> case of embarrassment, since this always calls
> forth a full display of the dancers' agility and gives
> much time.[66]

The dancer and the caller interact in a pattern similar to that of call and response in song; both patterns reflect African practices. The caller, invoking the dancers to ever-greater feats of endurance and virtuosity, recalls the African drummer who challenged and was challenged by ceremonial dancers. In some African cultures this interaction took the form of competition, a test of endurance; in plantation corn shuckings the caller may have required dance steps so rapid and complicated as to tax the dancers' skills, as Barrow implies: "Endurance is a strong point in the list of accomplishments of the dancer, and other things being equal, that dancer who can hold out the longest is considered the best."[67] By coordinating the dance movements, the caller also served an important social function. Since the participants were often from several plantations, each with its own dances, the caller helped create community consensus about the dance and made community participation possible. He either eliminated or integrated plantation particularisms to a general cultural standard.

The call and response typical of corn songs (and other slave songs) were deceptively simple, as the following lyric illustrates. The use of animal characters is typically African-American, and here the rabbit seems to be a metaphor for a slave trickster.

> Rabbit in de gyordin (*general's call*)
> Rabbit hi oh (*all hands respond*)
> Dog can't ketch um
> Rabbit hi oh
> Gun can't shoot um
> Rabbit hi oh
> Mon can't skin um

> Rabbit hi oh
> Cook can't cook um
> Rabbit hi oh
> Folks can't eat um
> Rabbit hi oh

The merriment of a corn shucking apparently included a good deal of amusement at the expense of unwitting slaveholders. The dances and the songs were often satirical, pointed instruments of criticism and resistance. A shucking song that tells of the master's good treatment seems on the surface to ridicule only the slaves from a neighboring plantation, but also hints at Jones's stinginess (or downright cruelty):[68]

> Massa's niggers am slick and fat
> Oh, Oh, Oh!
> Shine jes like a new beaver hat
> Oh, Oh, Oh!
> Turn out here and shuck dis corn,
> Oh, Oh, Oh!
> Biggest pile o' corn seen since I was born,
> Oh, Oh, Oh!
> Jones' niggers am lean an' po'
> Oh, Oh, Oh!
> Don't know whether dey get enough ter eat or no,
> Oh, Oh, Oh!

Slaves' dances served to deconstruct the imposing and powerful presence of whites. In the etiquette of slavery, blacks could not openly criticize whites, so dance was a safer tool for self-assertion, ridicule, and criticism than song. This use of dance was not confined to corn shuckings. Deriding whites through dance probably originated in dances of derision common to many African groups.[69] Whites either misconstrued these performances as simple foolishness or found some way to discount the comic imitation.

> It was generally on Sunday when there was little work . . . that the slaves both young and old would dress up in hand-me-down finery to do a high-kicking, prancing walk-around. They did a takeoff on the high manners of the white folks in the "big house," but their masters, who gathered around to watch the fun missed the point.[70]

Some whites, confident of their power, allowed slaves latitude in comedic performance. In some situations, authority was made to look small and insignificant, and whites were able to laugh off the disrespect. "The entertainment was opened by the men copying (or taking off) the manners of their masters and the women of their mistresses, and relating some highly curious anecdotes to the inexpressible diversion of that company."[71] Slaves used such occasions to assert personal dissatisfactions or communitywide complaints that would have drawn severe reactions in other contexts. African-American song and dance thus became entwined with resistance.

In this section we have seen that slave dances promoted community fellowship and consolidation and helped build cultural institutions. The institution of slavery included forces that worked against consolidation by creating status differences among slave workers. The dancing and other behaviors in these institutions were governed by a set of esthetic and technical principles further removed from their African origins than the dance activities already discussed. Such was the case with "slave balls," our next discussion.

Bals du Cordon Bleu

Communities of blacks were by no means monolithic. Free blacks enjoyed a higher status than slaves, and some categories of work conferred special status. Household service on plantations enjoyed greater prestige than field work, and artisans in urban areas were much more highly regarded than laborers. Similar distinctions operated among free blacks in cities. Some were so valued for their skills that they achieved local fame and whites took pride in having engaged them. Conversely, slaves took pride in the prestige of their owners. Author Samuel Mordecai[72] observed:

> The servants belonging to the old families in Virginia and especially those pertaining to domestic households, were as proud of their position as if the establishment was their own. The house servants acquired something of the polite and respectful demeanor which prevailed among the gentility. The coachman in an old family felt as proud of his position on the box as he could have felt had he been inside.
>
> The most prominent member of the black aristocracy of my early years was Sy Gilliat, (probably Simon or Cyrus) the leading violinist (fiddler was then the word), at balls and dancing parties. Sy Gilliat flourished in Richmond in the first decade of this century, and I know not how many of the last. His manners were as courtly as his dress.

Mordecai describes other members of the "slave aristocracy" of Richmond; including Mrs. Nancy Bryd, a pastry chef ("no dinner party nor supper could be complete unless Nancy had a finger in the pie"). He notes that these African-Americans imitated the social niceties of the white upper class.

> Like their betters, the negroes of the present day have their mock-gentility, and like them, they sustain it chiefly in dress and pretension. These gentry leave their visiting cards at each others' kitchens, and on occasions of a wedding, Miss Dinah Drippings and Mr. Cuffie Coleman have their cards connected by a silken tie, emblematic of that which is to connect themselves, and a third card announces, "at home from ten to one," where those who call will find cake, fruits and other refreshments.

Indeed, urban slaves used elaborate dress as a mark of their status. A visitor from New England was astonished

> to see slaves with broadcloth suits well fitted and nicely ironed fine shirts, polished boots, gloves, umbrellas for sunshade, the best of hats, their young men with their blue coats and bright buttons, in their latest style, white Marseilles vests, white pantaloons, brooches in their shirtbosoms, gold chains, elegant sticks and some old men leaning on their ivory and silver headed staves, as respectable in their attire as any who that day went to the House of God.[73]

The treatment of people of mixed race varied considerably. Sexual exploitation of slave women was common, resulting in a substantial number of mixed-race slaves. Although some slave owners took pains to conceal their transgressions by selling pregnant concubines, others allowed the mixed-race children to grow up as slaves alongside their legitimate offspring. Still others freed their concubines and children. Compared with the wholly bleak outlook for slave children, some of the master's mixed-race children could hope for freedom or at least a more comfortable life. For those who deeply resisted any connection with whites, a light complexion became a mark of potential outsider status; for those determined to make their lives (or their children's) more tolerable, light skin could be a social advantage. In time, color distinctions augmented work status in creating a complex social hierarchy:

> The variety in complexion, status and attainment among town slaves led to a somewhat elaborate gradation of colored society. One stratum comprised the fairly numerous quadroons and mulattoes along with certain exceptional blacks. The men among these had a pride of place as butlers and coachmen, painters and carpenters; the women fitted themselves trimly with the cast-off silks and muslins of their mistresses, walked with mincing tread, and spoke in quiet tones with impressive nicety of grammar. This element was a conscious aristocracy of its kind.[74]

While no caste system as such existed in the South, elite groups of free and enslaved African-Americans formed in southern cities such as New Orleans, Charleston, Louisville, Mobile, Montgomery, and Richmond. The cultural life of these groups bore little resemblance to that on the plantation. Plantation slaves described their dances as "balls," but these affairs had little of the genteel atmosphere and decorum that were a remarkable feature of the balls organized by slaves and quadroons in urban settings.

Author Eyre Crowe, who traveled with the British author Thackeray on his famous visit to the United States, leaves us this account of a ball held in Charleston, South Carolina, March 8, 1853:

> This rule of nocturnal retirement was obviously relaxed whenever a negro ball was given. We had the privilege of being invited to see one of these amusements. The saltatory features of the scene here given were quaint yet picturesque. The minstrels were embowered in greenery as they played waltzes and quadrilles, which were danced with great zest, and the hall rang with good-humored laughter.
>
> The refreshments were limited to spruce-beer, of which we drank thankfully, as administering a novel sensation to the jaded palate. The striking features of negro evening dress consisted in astonishing turbans with marabou feathers, into which add accessories of squib shape and other forms were inserted. [75]

The presence of white observers was not unusual; both the urban slave balls and plantation slave dances were attended by whites who served variously as social arbiters, onlookers, and participants.

> During the winter, the negroes in Montgomery, have their "assemblies," or dress balls, which are got up "regardless of expense," in a very grand style. Tickets to these balls are advertised, "admitting one gentlemen and two ladies," $1, and "ladies are assured that they may rely on the strictest order and propriety being observed."
>
> Cards of invitation, finely engraved with handsome vignettes, are sent, not only to the fashionable slaves, but to some of the more esteemed white people, who however, take no part, except as

lookers-on. All the fashionable dances are executed; no one is admitted, except in full dress:
there are the regular masters of ceremonies, floor
committees, etc.; and a grand supper always forms
a part of the entertainment. [76]

Whites exercised their rights of access at both
types of affairs, as Elen Campbell, a former slave from
Georgia, recalled: "Den sometimes on Saddy night we
have a big frolic. De nigger frum Hammond's place and
Phinizy place, Eve place, Clayton place, D'Laigle place
all git togedder fer big dance and frolic. A lot o de
young white sports used to come dere and push de
nigger bucks aside and dance wid de wenches."[77]

Campbell's testimony, as well as other evidence,
suggests that slave dances and balls were places where
white men sought romantic, sexual liaisons with
women of African descent. Women of mixed African
and European heritage were particularly prized for
these liaisons. In Louisiana, the presence of a large
mixed-blood population facilitated the development of
normalized sexual relationships with white men.
Charles Gayarre, Louisiana historian, creator of the
Louisiana state library, and magistrate of the New Orleans city courts in the early 1800s, describes the
growth of this population:

A census taken in 1788, this free mixt blooded
population numbered about 200 free blacks who in
that census may have been in the total of 1700 put
down as the number of that sort of population for
there were few emancipated negroes at that time.
From 1788 to 1809, twenty-one years, we calculate
that it may have increased 3,500. In that year,
1809, there arrived from the west indies, in conse-

quence of events in St. Domingo, and subsequently in Cuba, 1,977 mixed blooded and pure Africans. Excluding the full blooded blacks. We estimate that mixt blooded at 1,500 which number, added to 3,500 above mentioned, gives what we believe to be about a correct total of 5,000 mixed blooded, or *gens de couleur.* They probably had swelled to over 10,000 souls from 1825 to 1830—the epoch we select to represent their condition.[78]

That women of African ancestry were especially appealing to white men and that dances provided the opportunity for sexual alliances is indicated by a 1785 ordinance (Louisiana was still under Spanish domination) aimed at curbing the activities of quadroon women. They were forbidden to wear jewels and feathers, were ordered to have their hair bound in a kerchief, and were forbidden to have balls that were here referred to as "nightly assemblies."[79]

Beginning in French Louisiana and continuing until emancipation, particularly in the areas surrounding New Orleans, institutional concubinage known as *la placage,* or the placee system, developed. In a *placage* arrangement the couple, though not legally married, lived together as if they were. Though marriage between Indians, whites, and people of African descent was illegal, *la placage* became a permanent fixture of New Orleans and other regions of the antebellum South. In fact, it existed wherever there was slavery— Haiti, Dutch Guinea, Martinique, Guadeloupe, Jamaica, Peru, and Mexico.[80] An important element in its perpetuation in Louisiana was the quadroon ball.

Unlike other dances in which people of African descent took part, a quadroon ball was held specifically for wealthy white males to meet colored or mixed-blood women and acquire them as mistresses. These dances entailed elaborate public displays and ritualized exchanges; their elaborate formalization is characteristic of elite dancing. Although concubinage between white men and women of African descent was widespread, these sophisticated public occasions were peculiar to the New Orleans area, except for the "dignity" or "quality" balls of Barbados. Possibly slave balls in other areas served a similar function, but I have found no evidence to support such a conclusion. Numerous accounts indicate that these affairs were attended solely by wealthy white males and mulatto, quadroon, and octoroon women. The historical and more folkloric literature on Louisiana has little to say about them. The contemporary accounts describe them with such idealized romanticism that we know little about their evolution or what actually occurred at them.[81]

Gayerre and other sources imply that by 1788 colored balls and dances had become an important feature of social life in Louisiana. The mixed-blood free community, like slaves who attended balls in other areas, was primarily urban, and existed as a separate entity between the black slave and free white communities. Their ability to make modest economic and social progress distinguished them significantly from black slaves. In New Orleans these *gens de couleur,* particularly the women, "had their boxes at the Orleans theatre, wore diamonds, sported Parisian headdresses, rivalled white women in the elegance of their toilette."[82]

In the urban South the statutory regulations and

customs that supported strict segregation were selectively enforced, often blatantly violated—principally by white men. Free people of color enjoyed certain social privileges but were well aware that their liberties could be curtailed at any time. For example, on January 19, 1781, during the war between England and Spain, the city of New Orleans was filled with troops and crews of Spanish ships. Fearing for his ability to control the troops as well as large numbers of slaves and free per-. sons of color, the Spanish attorney general prohibited masking and the usual public dancing enjoyed by the nonwhite community, both slave and free. Moreover, quadroons could be relegated to a state of servitude at almost any time. A popular play of the period entitled *The Octoroon: or Life in Louisiana* testifies to their tenuous class stability. [83]

Many whites perceived the *gens de couleur* and free blacks as a threat to the hegemony of the slaveholder class. In 1788 "an excessive attention to dress" by a mulatto or quadroon was considered, according to the ordinance of Governor Miro, "as evidence of misconduct and made her liable to punishment." Little had changed by 1806 when the legislature of the Territory of Orleans adopted a statute forbidding slaves or free people of African descent to presume themselves "equal to the white."[84] In theaters, opera halls, and other public accommodations, the areas reserved for quadroons and free persons of color reflected their inferior status, and they were forbidden certain public behavior and attire. Even genteel colored families were forced to practice selective propriety in the homes of the New Orleans *gens de couleur;* "when the females of their families were visited by gentlemen of the dominant class, it was accepted etiquette for them [black men] never to be present."[85]

In short, the free mixing of the races was a one-way privilege; black males did not openly enter into liaisons with white women, nor did they patronize white celebrations. Whites, however, frequented colored taverns, public dance halls, and private dances and balls to such an extent that in February 1800, the Spanish attorney general, Pedro Barran, requested that the city reduce the number of public dance halls in an attempt to lessen disorder and better regulate race mixing.[86]

The nature of urban life, however, made the control of slaves, skilled slaves in particular, hard to accomplish. Bricklayers, engineers, barbers, midwives, blacksmiths, even druggists and trusted house servants received considerable latitude during their hours off and were often indistinguishable from their legally free brethren. In addition, they often had money for admission to public dance halls.[87]

New Orleans under Barran resolved to prohibit public colored dances and limit gatherings to private homes; whites were forbidden to attend these affairs. In response, Bernardo Coquet and his partner José Boniquet proposed to underwrite the city's unprofitable first theater, which had been losing money for the past decade, in exchange for the exclusive right to hold public dances for colored people. This arrangement was to last for one year under the following conditions: the partners could hold one dance every Sunday evening, two per week during carnival season; slaves would not be admitted without a written permit from their masters, and no other colored dances would be

allowed in the city. This arrangement seemed acceptable to all parties since it limited the number of
colored dances and saved the theater's operas and
dramas for the city. Soon after carnival season, however, the colored dances resumed admitting black and
white, slave and free. Complaints again followed that
"the dances often displayed luxury equally that of
white dances and that free people and slaves of both
sexes attended."[88] According to one exasperated
citizen,

> At the corners of all the cross streets of the city are
> to be seen nothing but taverns, which are open at
> all hours. There the canaille white and black, free
> and slave mingled, go openly and without any em-
> barrassment, as well as without shame to revel and
> dance indiscriminately and for whole nights with a
> lot of men and women of saffron color, or quite
> black, either free or slave. I will only designate the
> famous house of Coquet, located near the center of
> the city, where all scum is to be seen publicly and
> for several years—to that degree that the tricolor
> balls are not at all secret; I have several times seen
> the printed announcements posted at the street
> corners, with the express permission of the civil
> governor.[89]

The quadroon ball as such was born in 1805 when
Coquet rented his ballroom on St. Philip Street to
Auguste Tessier, an actor and dancer in the local
opera company, and moved his own dances to another
location. Tessier devised a sure-fire money-making
scheme. Beginning on Saturday, November 23, he
would give two balls a week, on Wednesday and Saturday, for free women of color; colored men would be

excluded. Tessier's experiment proved an enormous financial success and the quadroon ball soon became a major attraction of New Orleans. White men flocked to the balls for an introduction that might lead to a *placage*.[90]

> The men, particularly the planters and those whose
> business of life, carried on by slaves, left them considerable leisure, tired of the monotonous society of
> women of their own class and found their amusement in gambling and with the already large and
> dangerous class of quadroons. Of the attraction of
> the latter, many a foreign visitor has left glowing descriptions. Already the public balls arranged for
> them by enterprising managers were a chief institution of the town, and their gaiety and contrast to
> the monotony of the man-of-leisure's existence gave
> them a dangerous attraction against which other influences fought in vain.[91]

During the early days of American occupation in the first part of the nineteenth century, quadroon balls were being given in the famous Orleans Ballroom, which for years had been the scene of the most fashionable of white balls. By the 1830s as many as three balls a week were being given. The entrance fee for men was approximately $2—each gentlemen who attended paid a fee that was around twice that for the white balls and masquerades.[92] Thus, the quadroon ball emerged as the scheme of a dance-hall entrepreneur, not a spontaneous cultural development of the colored community.

The attraction of these peculiar social institutions were several. Frederick Law Olmsted seems to condone *placage* as a means by which frugal young men could live comfortably while making their way in the business world. Note his implication that white women's extravagance drove white men into the arms of black women, who had to earn their keep.

One reason which leads to this way of living to be frequently adopted by unmarried men, who come to New Orleans to carry on business, is, that it is much cheaper than living at hotels and boarding houses. As no young man ordinarily dare think of marrying, until he had made a fortune to support the extravagant style of house-keeping, and gratify the expensive tastes of young women, as fashion is now educating them, many are obliged to make up their minds never to marry. Such a one undertook to show me that it was cheaper for him to *placer* than to live in any other way that he could be expected to in New Orleans. He hired, at a low rent, two apartments in the older part of the town; his placee did not, except occasionally, require a servant; she did the marketing, and performed all the ordinary duties of house-keeping herself; she took care of his clothes, and in every way was economical and saving in her habits—it being her interest, if her affections for him were not sufficient, to make him as much comfort and as little expense as possible, that he might be more strongly attached to her, and have the less occasion to leave her. He concluded by assuring me that whatever might be said against it, it certainly was better than the way in which most young men lived who depended on salaries in New York. [93]

Why would women of African descent enter such relationships? For many, a more comfortable life; for others, the promise of freedom. White men sometimes protected their children from becoming slaves, and the child's fortune was often the mother's fortune. To white males, the appeal of *placage* was powerful on several levels. Interracial sexual relationships promised exotic, forbidden pleasures and freedom from the bounds of respectable behavior within the relationship. In a society in which all women were subjugated to men, no laws or conventions restricted the treatment of black women. Even free black women could be considered the property of their white male lovers and in many relationships, particularly with urban slaves, the man legally owned his mistress.[94] Though many men honored their responsibilities as fathers and "husbands," others ignored their responsibilities without penalty.

We can only surmise the attitude of the quadroon men toward these arrangements. The balls must have been a blatant reminder of their inferior status and powerlessness. No man of African ancestry was allowed to attend these celebrated affairs in any capacity other than menial or musician.[95]

These functions were essentially glorified slave marts. Mothers brought their thirteen- and fourteen-year-old daughters, dressed in their finery, and paraded them for inspection. Surveying a group of quadroon girls, the "patron" was virtually assured of the young woman's virginity. If he chose to pursue one, he made preliminary arrangements with her mother. After assuring the mother that he could indeed support her daughter in a fitting style, and having reached an understanding as to his obligations and duties, the man concluded the negotiations by presenting a gift or a house to the mother. The arrangements would include a financial plan for the girl and any children she might have. The patron was then permitted to call on the girl. After the two principals reached an agreement, a party was given and announcements made to friends. The girl then went to live with her "protector," frequently assuming his name. [96]

The frequency of quadroon balls and the testimony of contemporary observers indicate that by 1788 *placage* was widespread among those white males who could afford it. Predictably, critics mourned the decline of morality and regarded miscegenation as a threat to white supremacy. In 1788 Governor Estevan Miro issued (to little effect) his *Bando de buen gobierno,* article 5 of which was specifically directed against concubinage with women of African descent. White women in particular clamored for an end to the balls, and in 1828 successfully pressured the city council to adopt an ordinance that forbade white men with or without masks to attend balls with women of color. [97]

Little changed as a result of the ordinance, but other forces were at work to undermine quadroon balls. One was the growing discontent with slavery. The quadroon balls depended on the meager privilege granted to quadroons and "people of color," as distinct from enslaved Africans; as the slave system drew increasing opposition, lines were more sharply drawn and the fine points of racial distinctions blurred.

After the 1830s, the peak era for these dances, the social status of the free black and colored community diminished. The 1850s were particularly noteworthy for legislative decrees and prejudicial writings that challenged the status of free people of African descent and *gens de couleur.* The growing hostility was reflected in local newspapers. A free man of color judged guilty of insulting a policeman was fined $25, but the *Daily Picayune* thought twenty-five lashes more appropriate so as "to teach him the difference between white and brown." Free Negroes "are not a desired population and they may be a dangerous one." In some communities, according to Sterks, the anti-African sentiment gave rise to vigilante committees determined "to prevent slave insurrections and immoral conduct between White men and free colored women. . . . On one occasion the Lafayette Parish Vigilantes whipped a white man named Auguste Gudbeer and his free mulatress mistress, and they gave the unfortunate couple eight days to leave the parish."[98]

The quadroon balls declined in this hostile atmosphere, and by the Civil War their eradication was nearly complete. During the war so many young men left home to fight for the Confederacy that few girls had "protectors."[99] After the war, all persons of African heritage were equal under the law. In practice this meant that all were subject to the full range of discrimination.

While the quadroon ball disappeared after emancipation, the other slave balls and traditions of gentility flourished. The new social and political relations between blacks and whites provided conditions in which new dance arenas could emerge.

SHODDY CONFINES: THE JOOK CONTINUUM

Singing and playing in the true Negro style is
called jooking.
—Zora Neal Hurston, 1934

The Great Transition

THERE was no autonomous social life under slavery.
Whether slave owners did or did not control specific
activities, they had the power to do so. Generally they
granted or withdrew social privileges as a means of
controlling work productivity. Living in plantation
slave quarters, however, fostered the sense of a community, distinctly African in flavor. This sense of
community existed in a dynamic tension with white
control and allowed for the creation of distinctly
African-American cultural activities.

Under bondage slaves danced whenever they could,
both openly and surreptitiously; often any space or
shelter would do—barns, sugar refineries, jails, praise
houses. In the Reconstruction era, some African-
Americans, now responsible for their own upkeep and
cultural activities, regarded mobility as an expression

of their emancipation and headed for the nearest urban center. [1] Some were frightened by their new freedom. In any case, the breakup of large plantations and the destruction of the slave quarter prevented owners from maintaining a large company of servants and field hands. Never again would the vast majority of African-Americans find themselves in such homogeneous communities.

Life in slave quarters offered some insulation from white culture; it enabled African-Americans to transform their cultural activities, especially the dance, into a complexly woven facet of their lives. The system of rhythmically ordered gesture signified, particularly through its use of themes of derision, the slave community's concern for social morality. The dances also performed an educational function. They provided a language through which slaves could comment on work and on the behavior of whites and other slaves. Dance also helped organize behavior. For example, slaves used ostracism from clandestine dances to sanction each other's behavior. A former slave provides an illustration. As a child he was taken to a clandestine dance. Later he was forced by his master to tell the names of those who had participated: "I knew it was wrong but I did so to save my hide. Nobody got any whipping though, but it was the last time I got to go along with them to a frolic."[2]

In the slave quarters, distinctions between family and community relations blurred. The continual auctioning off and acquisition of new slaves created fluidity, although this impermanence was offset to some degree by the commonalities of plantation life. Shared privation encouraged strong bonds of loyalty, which included sharing limited goods, protecting the weak, and respecting each other's property.[3] In highest esteem was the "code of silence" that forbade slaves to give whites information about each other. According to Charles C. Jones, a Georgia planter,

the Negroes are scrupulous on one point; they make common cause as servants in concealing their faults from their owners. Inquiry elicits no information; no one feels at liberty to disclose the transgressor, the matter assumes the sacredness of a "professional secret:" for they remember that they may hereafter require the same concealment of their own transgressions from their fellow servants, and if they tell upon them now, they may have the like favor returned them besides, in the meanwhile, having their names cast out as evil from among their brethren, and being subjected to scorn and perhaps personal violence or pecuniary injury.[4]

Frederick Douglass makes a similar point:

We were as true as steel, and no band of brothers could have been more loving. There were no mean advantages taken of each other, no tattling; no giving each other bad names, and no elevating one at the expense of the other. We were generally a unit, and moved together.[5]

Although the circumstances of slavery encouraged silence, composure, and self-control, these traits have long been valued in African culture. Among the Nigerian Yoruba and Cuban Lucumi one can observe the "code of silence" in its religious context. Yoruba sculpture frequently portrays "sealed lips." In Cuba the code is exemplified by the *sese* drum of Abakuá. This drum is not played, but remains "an instrument of significant silence."[6]

By and large slavery inhibited the retention of African culture. While the ultimate power on all matters lay outside the slave community, slaves could not establish a durable social normative system. Only in that unregulated sociocultural space mentioned in our discussion of the plantation environment did slaves have the power to develop community norms or sanction individual transgressions.

Emancipation forced enormous changes in rural black life. African-Americans were dispersed into separate living quarters, with each family responsible for its own upkeep. Many were barely able to survive in these radically changed circumstances. Increased autonomy should have allowed for a more varied social life for African-Americans, but whites successfully continued to restrict most facets of their lives. White landowners drew up labor contracts that forbade the workers to gather or to journey away from the plantation without the owner's permission. Other contracts forbade nighttime gatherings. White-run local governments passed health ordinances to control the flow of freedmen into the cities; smallpox ordinances were partly designed to do just that. Many who wished to celebrate holidays in the city or spend a day off there were prevented from traveling. In cooperation with landowners, some municipalities passed legislation forbidding entry to freedmen without written permission of their employer. Thus, landowners tried to maintain control over the black work force even as they were relieved of the responsibilities that accompanied such control. The restrictions on freedmen were little more than the old black codes restated, with *Negro* or *servant* replacing the word *slave*.[7]

Nevertheless, African-Americans moved around considerably. Since many lacked the job skills needed in urban areas, they sought agricultural jobs from plantation to plantation under the contract system. Whether because they were dissatisfied with working conditions or were forced off the land without pay for their work (as frequently happened), this unprecedented large-scale movement helped to further homogenize many remaining regional cultural variations.

African-American traveling performers also contributed to cultural standardization. As black entertainers crisscrossed the South in tent shows, medicine shows, and gillies, they disseminated vocabulary, toasts, rhymes, music, and dance. Dances such as the snake hips, cakewalk, Texas tommy, Virginny breakdown, black bottom, Charleston, and Georgia hutch probably gained initial acclaim among African-Americans through these entertainers, who should not be confused with white minstrels:

> While the large white minstrel companies exploded into gigantic irrelevancies, Negro minstrels persisted on a smaller scale in the South. Luckily, it was forced to do precisely what it could do best. With dancing talent but without the financial resources to imitate the excesses of the white companies, Negro minstrels tailored its entertainment to rural audiences in the South and kept its size and format as a small carnival or gilly with a Jig Top.[8]

Emancipation enabled blacks to re-create their own culture openly, but new centers for black social life were needed to accomplish that. By the time of Reconstruction, the sacred and the secular existed in separate spheres in African-American culture. New cultural institutions, of both types, flowered in the black community. Economic and social needs inspired the proliferation of private voluntary associations and benevolent societies that provided for such benefits as economic support, mutual aid in "sickness and distress," life insurance, and proper burials. Their very names point to their symbolic importance: Knights and Daughters of I Will Rise; Order of Lone Star Race Pride, Friendship, Love and Help; the Grand United Order of True Reformers; United Brothers of Friendship; Sisters of the Mysterious Ten; Samaritans. Some of these organizations predated emancipation. The Free African Union Society of Providence, Rhode Island, and the Free African Society of Philadelphia were established in the 1780s by free African-Americans. By 1848 there were 106 of these societies functioning in Philadelphia, with a membership of 8,000.[9]

After 1870, as black communities grew in the North and in southern cities, so did membership and activities of such organizations as the Elks, Masons, Eastern Star, and Odd Fellows; it was the golden age of secret societies. The True Reformers, organized in Richmond, Virginia, in 1881, was the most remarkable secret society of the period. Between 1881 and 1901 it paid out $600,000 in death claims and $1,500,000 in sick benefits; its membership numbered over 50,000. It maintained a bank with over $500,000 in assets, a mercantile and industrial association that did an annual business of over $100,000, a weekly newspaper with a printing department, a hotel with accommodations for 150 guests, an old folks home, an incorporated building and loan association, and a real estate department with property valued at $400,000.[10]

In the years after emancipation, schools for African-Americans sprang up, and the church became the primary organizer of religious and some social activities for blacks, but their influence on the direction and character of working-class African-American institutional social life was limited. The secular cultural organizations were primarily urban; some of them, originally church related, experienced a tremendous growth after emancipation. All in all, however, the new options for black culture were not realized in ways that were of significant benefit to the black community. The commercialized entertainments that swept across the country were largely controlled by profiteers and politicians.

Before the Civil War, free African-Americans in cities had generated an independent cultural tradition centered on political struggle for emancipation. They founded African free schools, African union societies, literary clubs, and black newspapers. These developments were manifestations of the community's desire for "race betterment." During the postemancipation era, "race improvement" continued to motivate the advantaged segments of the black community. They raised money for primary, secondary, and college education, for orphanages, for benevolent causes, and later for the families of lynch victims.[11] African-American organizations, including lodges such as the Odd Fellows, Prince Hall Masons, and many others, sponsored numerous dances and soirees for benevolent causes. Private benefits known as balls were also common.

The "race improvement" dances were distinct from those held by country freedmen. The tone of the affairs, choice of dances, and musical accompaniment more closely paralleled white dances. Emancipation intensified this social differentiation. The activities of the black upper strata signified an acceptance of white upper-class cultural hegemony, and the dances at the race improvement affairs had a distinctly European flavor. No African-inspired dances, no congo or buzzard lope, were performed in these arenas. Socially elite blacks danced in a "dizzying round of quadrilles, waltzes, continental, Prince Imperials varieties, New Yorks, pinafore lancers, polkas, mazurkas, valses, cotillions, grand marches and schottisches often until early morning."[12]

These public dances, particularly those with interracial sponsorship, served to acculturate blacks moving into the middle-class, urban lifestyle. For the first time (with the possible exception of antebellum cities such as Richmond, New Orleans, and Montgomery), a large class of free African-Americans had access to European elements in American culture.

Other nineteenth-century celebrations included all members of the community, elite and nonelite alike. A staple event was the Emancipation Day celebration. These affairs were popular in practically every African-American community, particularly after 1865, although several were celebrated before then. Jerry Rescue Day, a local event in Syracuse, New York, began on October 1, 1851, when a group of white citizens freed a slave named Jerry and sent him to Canada.

The tenor of these events reflected the region in which they occurred. April 16, 1862, marked the end of slavery in Washington, D.C., and it was commemorated in grand style. The local newspaper *The Bee* carried a description of the twenty-first anniversary celebration. It included a street parade a mile and a half long, with 150 carriages in line and at least 40 different delegations representing social clubs, voluntary associations, secret societies, legislative districts, minstrel troops, national guard divisions, drill and military groups, several parade "queens," labor and trade organizations, and musicians, and featured the Honorable Frederic Douglass as the orator of the day. *The Cleveland Gazette* in 1886 carried an advertisement for an emancipation celebration:

> Grand Emancipation Celebration by the Colored People of Youngstown, O. on Tuesday, August 3, 1886. The exercises will consist of music by the different bands, singing, speaking and dancing in a spacious hall. The grand feature will be the Emancipation Ball in the evening at the Great Western Rink with a dancing capacity for 500 couples. Music by the American Orchestra of Pittsburgh.[13]

Festivities in the South more directly reflected their African heritage. Drum dancing was an important part of the May Emancipation Day celebrations in Georgia, Florida, Alabama, and Mississippi. According to informants, blacks in east Mississippi celebrated their freedom by beating drums, singing, and "dancing all night." Similarly, celebrants in Alabama formed "line walks" and danced to the beating of drums. Drums, both large and small, were played by old men who would periodically stop as they moved through the crowd; people would form a circle and individuals would "jump in the circle and dance."[14]

Many secular celebrations dropped in popularity by the 1940s, except for Juneteenth, the most durable of them all. Juneteenth apparently began on June 19, 1865, when General Gordon Granger and Union troops landed in Galveston, Texas, announcing the end of slavery. The Emancipation Proclamation had little effect in Texas before that, because there were few northern troops to enforce it. The Juneteenth celebrations, which spread throughout the Southwest, typically included a parade, complete with floats, marching bands, and parade queen. But the most impressive symbols in the early parades were former slaves who walked at the end of the march. The Juneteenth celebrations included a picnic barbecue, fish fry, sports events such as baseball, and, in certain regions of Texas, a rodeo.[15]

The guest speakers at most Emancipation Day festivities were skilled in the African-American tradition of oratory. Known throughout black America as "race men," they were proud of their blackness and actively engaged in the struggle for black freedom and racial uplift. Until 1900 these celebrations served a variety of functions, including local fund raising to aid widows, orphans, and the less well-off members of various communities.[16] Communitywide participation was common, but the upper-strata voluntary organizations and social clubs dominated events that featured social dancing.

With the official end of Reconstruction in 1877 and the withdrawal of federal troops from the South, a formal policy of segregation and franchise restrictions was developed to check the aspirations of African-Americans. Widespread vigilante violence, whether gratuitous or in response to a minor or trumped-up offense, made a mockery of freedom. Lynchings became so common that citizens all over the country demanded the end of white mob rule. The violence continued virtually unabated until after the middle of this century.

The terrorism, coupled with an economic depression in the South, fueled a black migration. Although a few were able to leave for the West Indies or Africa, most people headed for urban areas. Many went north where new industrial jobs were opening up. Northern manufacturers, to meet the ever-increasing demand for goods, turned to African-American laborers when by 1916 the influx of European immigrant laborers declined. They advertised for workers in black newspapers and sent recruiters south. Providing free train tickets and promising good jobs, these agents directed large numbers of black workers to industrial centers like Cleveland, Detroit, and Chicago. The black population of Cleveland quadrupled in ten years, from 8,448 in 1910 to 34,451 in 1920; three-quarters of that increase resulted from migration between 1916 and 1919. [17]

Seeking to grow with this soaring population, black newspapers like the *Chicago Defender* provided support services to newly arrived immigrants. The *Defender* sponsored fund drives for needy families and attempted to inculcate middle-class standards, offering prizes, for example, for well-kept yards. It also carried listings of job opportunities, housing, and other significant advertisements. [18]

In northern cities such as Chicago, Cleveland, Detroit, New York, and Philadelphia, the established social elites continued to give dances and affairs for charitable purposes, and their social events largely resembled those in the genteel South. Private benevolent organizations—Elks, Masons, Odd Fellows—were the major sponsors. These clubs became a mainstay of the urban elite. While "old family" membership became a less significant feature of such clubs, other forms of restriction took hold. New clubs maintained both class and caste stratification, and the rigidity of their admission policies was rivaled only by that of white groups. For example, members of Cleveland's Social Circle (which in 1904 became the Euchre Club) did not socialize with darker-skinned, less-educated members of Cleveland's growing "new elite." The Caterers Club, an elite group formed in 1903, gave a yearly banquet and ball and was likewise restrictive. Upper-strata social clubs and literary societies—the Chicago Old Settler's Club (1902), Appomattox Club (1900), the Manasseh Society—also reflected the growing class delineations. [19]

Similarly organized groups formed in Detroit around 1890. The Summer Club, modeled after the mostly white Michigan Club, forbade its members to indulge in such working-class entertainments as card playing, gambling, and drinking. The Oak and Ivy Club's founding membership was composed almost entirely of college graduates. These clubs, all with overlapping memberships, were collectively described as the "colored 150," or the "cultured colored 40 families." Their members prided themselves on avoiding popular dances, preferring to appear only at their own club's events.[20] The public dances of the black elite were modeled on white upper- and middle-class balls, and the prominent dances on these occasions were the waltz and the polka. Occasionally a subdued cakewalk might be performed, but African influences were generally shunned.

As the northern black community grew and diversified, distinctions of class and skin shade became more entrenched:

> You don't want me to start talking about the social life of Negroes in this town. Child, they are something! You see, we are always asking the white man to accept us when we won't even accept our own. When I first came to this city before 1917, if you didn't have the kiss of God, light skin, well you weren't accepted into anything.[21]

Alongside the developing network of lodges, social clubs, and voluntary organizations, black churches attempted to provide for the social life of their constituency. They sponsored picnics, balls, dances, and socials. Some black churches opposed other urban institutions that sponsored dancing. Although various groups within the church, such as the missionary society or young men's association, arranged dances (an "after Lenten dance," for example), these never assumed the status of institutions.[22] The "ball of racial uplift" evolved into a model for black elite society, and its format and objectives have remained intact for more than 130 years.

But despite the best efforts of the urban elite, black core culture was changing. As huge numbers of rural African-Americans migrated to northern cities, they brought with them customs forged in the rural South.

An informant recalled what Cleveland was like prior to 1917: "There were no barbeque joints and storefront churches or jook joints up here until all these Negroes came from down South. Oh, there were a few places way downtown but none to speak of, not like today."[23]

The Euro-American tradition was largely stagnant. In music and dance, the seeds of the future lay in the African past. Simultaneously, a third institution was emerging, different from both the sacred tradition and the traditions of the black elite. It became the fundamental formation from which all independent community dance arenas would derive their style and format. The African-American jook may very well be the most significant development in American popular dance and popular music history.

Jook Houses, Honky-Tonks, After-Hours Joints

Jooks, honky-tonks, and after-hours joints are secular institutions of social interaction and entertainment, usually associated with some quasilegal activity such as liquor sales or gambling. Their emergence was linked initially to peasant-class African-American life, and they appeared as soon as black populations became significant in both northern and southern towns. Basically, they are similar to night clubs. To the cursory observer the jook, the honky-tonk, and the after-hours joint may seem one and the same, but there are important subtle differences. In any case, *jook* is a more general label, since the honky-tonk and the after-hours joint may be classed as types of jooks.

On the plantation, blacks had become accustomed

to recreation that occurred largely in secrecy, away from whites. Precisely because gatherings of slaves or free people of African descent were illegal, slavery fostered black social institutions that defied white control, and thus helped create a recurrent pattern of covert social activity.[24] During the post-Reconstruction era, African-Americans saw a need—and an opportunity—to relocate the clandestine social activities and dances of the plantation days. Their freedom, the reorganized labor system, and their cultural past determined the shape of the first secular cultural institution to emerge after emancipation—the jook. Like the blues, the jook gave rise to and rejuvenated a variety of cultural forms. And, like the blues, the jook was a secular institution rooted in West African traditions that intertwined religious and secularized elements.

Following a sinuous evolutionary path shaped by history, motor-muscle memory, esthetic preference, and community reinforcement, "jookin'" first appeared in a format with precursors in West African religious celebration. Joyously ecstatic forms of worship, typical of African rites, undoubtedly survived among African-Americans. In the New World, however, the secular tended to separate from the sacred. The practices and remnants of institutional forms, such as "the party for the gods," took on a secular existence. In these joyous, often raucous celebrations, the jook format as well as its music and dance originated.

The separation of secular and sacred was not radical, however; there were, and still are, instances where the strands join again. Even today many African-American secular vocalists have a strong background in religious music and alternate between the two. Prominent examples include Thomas A. Dorsey (the father of modern gospel music, who also sang the blues),[25] Sam Cooke, Al Greene, Aretha Franklin, the Impressions, Marvin Gaye, Gladys Knight, Tina Turner, James Brown, Little Richard, and the Staple Singers. Even vocalists who have not emerged from black church choirs have some contact with gospel music.

My own observations indicate that influence flows in the other direction as well. As a child growing up in Cleveland, Ohio, in the 1950s and early 1960s, I often peered through the doors of a fundamentalist storefront Church of God in Christ during their midweek evening praise services. Frequently, amid the sounds of tambourines, bongos, saxophone, and piano, both the dance and music became virtually indistinguishable from those in the local after-hours joints. Neighbors frequently commented on the similarity. We could hear the same chord progressions, call-and-response patterns, implied polyrhythms, and use of falsetto and melisma. Dances that secular performers called the mashed potatoes, the shout, and the jerk were being performed in praise of God. Add food and fellowship, substitute gambling and drinking for the prayers and reverence, and you have all the ingredients necessary for "jookin'."

Jooking certainly occurred in the plantations, and even there, particularly for outsider observers, the celebration seemed to blend sacred and secular elements. The spaces used for these events typically housed various activities. Jails, sugar refineries, barns, open-air spaces, and praise houses—all were used for secular parties and religious services at one time or another. When questioned about their dancing during religious services, slaves frequently replied that they were not dancing at all, but "shouting." Though the physical movement was often the same, slaves felt some pressure to draw a distinction between the two. Wals Wilson, a Louisiana slave, explained the difference: "Us 'longed to de church, all right, but dancin' ain't sinful iffen de foots ain't crossed. Us danced at de arbor meetin's but us sho' didn't have us foots crossed."[26] As African-Americans moved more closely toward a European or American lifestyle, the separations became more clearly defined.

Zora Neal Hurston defined the jook as "the word for a Negro pleasure house. It may mean a bawdy house. It may mean the house set apart on public works where men and women dance, drink, and gamble. Often it is a combination of all these." Johnny Shines, a Mississippi Delta musician who played music in numerous jooks, commented, "The town was loaded with musicians. And lots of places to play there too. Juke joints I'd guess you'd call them. Now, a juke joint is a place where people go to play cards, gamble, drink, and so on. So far as serving drinks like you would in a bar or tavern no, it wasn't like that. Beer was served in cups; whiskey you had to drink out of a bottle."[27]

The etymology of *jook* is uncertain. The first to examine the term was Lorenzo D. Turner, who concluded that it probably derived from the West African Bambara word *dzugu,* meaning wicked or violent. Another theory is that *jook* derived from the West African Bamana-kan term *jugu,* which means bad. According to scholar Robert Farris Thompson:

There is even a phrase in Bamana-kan, *a kagni
jugu* literally "he good ba-a-ad" which has such an
up-to-date ring in black America for good historical
reasons of linguistic continuity through relexifica-
tion. In other words, *jugu* may have been replaced
by "bad" by the first or second generation of plantation speakers but the nuance and linguistic gravy
remain. Of course juke-box therefore translates
back as b-a-a-d-box and even calling a musical instrument a "box" shows the gravitational pull of
some language I haven't identified yet but it's there,
I'm sure. [28]

Otto and Burns contend that *jook* or *juke* has entered the vocabulary of white dialects of Georgia and
northern Florida. Whites use it as a verb—to go "juck-
ing," or go partying. [29] I have heard the term similarly
used in black communities in both North and South.
To add to this linguistic confusion, there are oc-
togenarians who refer to the first coin-operated music
machines and even electric guitars as "juice boxes" because they were plugged in to "the juice," the electric
current. In this book I will use *jook.*

The classic jook, though it might have been found
in a small town or even a city, catered to the rural work
force that began emerging after emancipation. Jooks
were often "shoddy confines," smelly and rarely im-
maculate. The term itself connotes a place where
lower-class African-Americans drink, dance, eat, and
gamble. Its constituency imposed a character and psy-
chology, derived from their labor experience, on the
first dance arena to emerge after emancipation. These
early jooks saw the first large-scale cross-fertilization
of dances, as thousands of freedmen sharecroppers as

well as traveling entertainers migrated from towns and faraway regions searching for employment.[30]

Even though the jook emerged during Reconstruction, its most intense development occurred in post-Reconstruction before the mass migration to the industrial North—that period when African-Americans were terrorized, lynched, and excluded from public life. With the intensification of white supremacy, African-Americans were more separated from mainstream American life than ever before. The reign of terror forced the black community into a tightly knit cultural group. It was during this period that the dances of working- and lower-class blacks relinquished some of their Euro-American characteristics.

Two trends in preemancipation dancing intensified in the post-Reconstruction jook houses. First, dance steps once linked to ritualistic or religious dancing now acquired a more firmly rooted secular identity. Second, group dance forms gave way to individual or partner dancing. Both changes can be observed in the popular dance of the 1920s, the big apple. Something resembling the big apple, with its counterclockwise circling and high arm gestures, appeared on plantations in South Carolina and Georgia before 1860, where it was known as the "ring shout." A group dance, the ring shout was associated with religious observance; the big apple, which derived from it, was a secular, individual dance. The shout, a popular dance of the 1950s, also derives from religious plantation dancing, but the shout maintained both its religious and secular identity.[31]

The jook was the only dance arena of its time that successfully accommodated the emerging regional culture among black freedmen. It served as a mixing ground for the remaining strains of African culture and those additional elements that developed during the slave experience. It provided a forum for blending regional and Euro-American cultural elements.[32] It later provided a forum for visitors or travelers to demonstrate new dances or variations, as well as an arena in which whites could observe and assimilate some aspects of black culture and dance. And it allowed African-Americans to express aspects of their newly developing national character.

Jooks were generally black owned and, although landowners expressed some concern about laborers' social activity, their ability to regulate it was limited. Technically, freedmen could "jook" every night if they wanted, stopping by after work for drinking and fellowship, an option that had not existed under bondage. Some of the activity in the jook required monetary exchange—gambling and purchasing food and beverages—and this contributed to the formation of an underground cultural and recreational network. There was a constant, if limited, flow of cash in and out of the jooks that eventually supported the famous "chittlin' circuit" on which many African-American musicians worked.

Zora Neal Hurston describes music typical of the jook:

> In past generations the music was furnished by "boxes," another word for guitars. One guitar was enough for a dance; to have two was considered excellent. Where two were playing one man played the lead and the other seconded him. The first was "picking" and the second was "framing," that is

playing chords while the lead carried the melody by
dexterous finger work. Sometimes a third player
was added, and he played a tom-tom effect on the
low strings. Believe it or not this is excellent dance
music. . . .
　　Musically speaking, the Jook is the most important place in America. For in its smelly shoddy confines has been born the secular music known as
the blues, and on blues has been founded jazz. The
singing and playing in the true Negro style is called
'jooking.' The songs grow by incremental repetition
as they travel from mouth to mouth and from Jook to
Jook for years before they reach outside ears. Hence
the great variety of subject-matter in each song. [33]

Music was initially provided by guitar, but "pianos
soon came to take the place of boxes and now player-
pianos and victrolas are in all the Jooks."[34]

　In jook joints and honky-tonks, African-American
dance culture crystallized into exportable forms. For
unlike the plantation frolics, the jooks and honky-
tonks were almost always open and the dancing was
free. The dance halls of the period, although public,
were to some degree restrictive, and brothels and saloons had a different focus. It was the jook and its derivative forms that provided black lower and working
classes with the primary public arena for dance.

　Dances in the jooks included the Charleston, the
shimmy, the snake hips, the funky butt, the twist, the
slow drag, the buzzard lope, the black bottom, the
itch, the fish tail, and the grind.[35] Most of these trace
back to Africa and can be observed there today (well as
in African and African-American communities around
the world). For example, scratching is part of West Af-

rican ceremonial dance to the god Legba, "guardian of the crossroads." Melville Herskovits observed a dance of the Winti people in Suriname in which dancers tug at their clothing as though scratching. This gesture became a standard routine known as the "itch" in black American social dancing; in tap dancing it was accompanied by eccentric footwork. By the late 1940s the itch had been incorporated into the breakaway of the lindy hop. It turned up again as an embellishment in the rhythm and blues dances of the 1950s.[36] I observed it in 1982 as part of a modern dance concert performed by Bill T. Jones and Arnie Zane. And so we have an African dance that reemerged in the southern jooks and from there into the contemporary setting and eventually onto the modern dance stage.

B. B. King, renowned blues guitarist and singer, remembers that advertisement for the jook was primarily word of mouth; the jook owner told his friends and they told theirs. Since some activity in the jooks was illegal and the early constituency primarily semi-literate, newspapers and posters were of limited use. In any case, jook joints usually held groups of only forty or fifty, so advertisements designed to bring in large crowds were unnecessary.[37]

The honky-tonk was the first urban manifestation of the jook, and the name itself later became synonymous with a style of music. Related to the classic blues in tonal structure, honky-tonk has a tempo that is slightly stepped up. It is rhythmically suited for many African-American dances including the funky butt, the slop, and the snake hips, later known as "poppin' the hips"; all require hip movement on a variety of planes.

Something resembling the modern-day honky-tonk first existed in urban centers like New Orleans, Memphis, Charleston, Mobile, and Birmingham. Early musicians like Jelly Roll Morton describe each city they worked as having a "tenderloin" district where illegal liquor sales, saloons, gambling, prostitution, and night life were the distinguishing features. "The saloons closed at 1:00 but that didn't make no difference, they just pulled down the shades." Gambling and illegal sales of liquor were the primary sources of support:

> Honky tonks had gambling rooms in the back; almost every place had gambling. Gambling was wide open. Always had an old broke down piano with some inferior pianist. Kaisers and Thanos in New Orleans were twenty-four hour honky tonks. Attendants were low women. The men were lousy. The main intake was from the gambling—a sucker would come in—always had some kind of gambling. The attendants came in after dark, that's when they got busy.[38]

The honky-tonk developed almost simultaneously with the jook house. The primary difference was in the patrons they served. In honky-tonks where Jelly Roll Morton played, "[you'd] see all kind of people come through these joints—longshoremen, roustabouts, cowboys. Yankees and every kind of woman in the world."[39] Unlike jook participants, most honky-tonk participants neither farmed for themselves nor sharecropped; they were wage laborers outside the agricultural routine, such as iron workers, loggers, and railroad laborers. However, rural African-Americans also went into town to the honky-tonks, giving the honky-tonk a character more heterogeneous than the classic jook. Frequently the rural patron's regular Saturday shopping excursion included an evening of entertainment in the local honky-tonk. Historian Hortense Powdermaker describes the process:

> On Saturdays colored tenants come to shop, to look about, to gossip with their friends. This is their chance to enjoy a social time after the week's work and the Negroes especially make the most of it. Wagons and old automobiles loaded with people drive in. Men and women crowd the dry goods stores, merely looking around if they are not able or ready to buy. All the people from the Negro section come uptown and the other streets are deserted. People loiter on the corners near the colored shops and the post office, talking and laughing. The colored restaurant is full. The evening is always a gala occasion celebrated by whiskey, music and dancing.[40]

Honky-tonks were viewed by some participants as places to make money, either through gambling or prostitution; in this respect they differed from the jook.

Though the dancing in the honky-tonks and the jooks was similar, it differed somewhat because the honky-tonks played more sophisticated music. More varied in style, it included not only blues, but ragtime and early jazz. Indeed, basic changes from the rural plantation blues style took place in the honky-tonks. They used more instruments and a greater variety, each instrument became more specialized. There was an increasing emphasis on narrative lyrics rather than phrases linked together around a general theme. Honky-tonks in larger cities like New Orleans also occasionally hired string trios or quartets.[41]

Dancing occupied a fair amount of African-Americans' leisure time in the late nineteenth and early twentieth centuries. Dances such as the black bottom, the Charleston, and the eagle rock became crazes that spread from jooks and honky-tonks to white America. According to Marshall and Jean Stearns, "the Black Bottom was a well-known dance among semiurban Negro folk in the South long before 1919."[42] The shimmy, truckin', and the cakewalk were also popular dances of the period. Most retained their popularity among African-Americans after World War I.

The dances performed in honky-tonks were part of a cultural cycle, many of whose elements resurfaced years later. For example, the leg gestures of the Charleston returned in the late 1950s and early 1960s as the mashed potatoes. The hip gestures of the black bottom returned as a dance embellishment in the lindy hop and jitterbug, appeared later as the mooche, and even later as a popular dance of the late 1960s and early 1970s, the four corners. This cyclical re-emergence continues to mark the African-American dance vocabulary.[43]

On the plantation, some dance gestures related to work tasks, such as "shuckin' corn" or "pitchin' hay." But little if any direct relationship between labor and dance existed in the honky-tonk. In the atmosphere of increasing urban anonymity and the pleasures of a good time, dance in the honky-tonk became more directly associated with sensation and sexual coupling. Performer Coot Grant, born in 1893, describes the

dances she observed in her father's Birmingham
honky-tonk in 1901:

> I had already cut out a peephole in the wall so I
> could watch the dancers in the back room. They
> did everything. I remember the Slow Drag, of
> course, that was very popular—hanging on each
> other and just barely moving. Then they did the
> Fanny Bump, Buzzard Lope, Fish Tail, Eagle Rock,
> Itch, Shimmy, Squat, Grind, Moche, Funky Butt
> and a million others. And I watched and imitated all
> of them. [44]

The slow drag spread far and wide in the semiurban honky-tonks known as barrelhouse joints. Pianist
Buster Pickens, who played the circuit, remembers:
"Up and down the Sante Fe tracks in those days was
known as the barrel-house joints, they danced all
night long. People that attended them were working at
the mill. It would take a couple of rooms, maybe a
store. The Dirty Dozens was the open' number. It settled down to the slow low down blues and they'd 'slow
drag.'"[45]

If the honky-tonk was more sophisticated than
the classic jook, it was less urbane than after-hours
joints. As their name suggests, these establishments
were willing to stay open after other places closed in
accord with the law. After-hours joints ranged widely
in decor and atmosphere, but most offered drinking,
dancing, music, food, and sometimes gambling. The
after-hours joint is more recent than the jook or the
honky-tonk, and came into being along with state licensing. Like the jook and honky-tonk, it occupies a
specific sociological space. The sociohistorical forces

that shaped it are slightly different from those that affected earlier forms.

The after-hours joint was in one sense a business establishment, a characteristic it shared with saloons, honky-tonks, and dance halls. Few charged an admission price, but once inside the participants were expected to pay for practically everything. Only the dancing came free, at least until coin-operated music appeared. Before the invention of jukeboxes, the source of music ranged from individual musicians to piano rolls and old Victrolas. A musician's services could always be enlisted for a plate of food or drinks; sometimes musicians would play for free.[46]

Almost anyone could convert part of a dwelling to an after hours-joint by clearing a space for dancing and music and providing seating, usually with tables. If someone owned a two-story house, the first floor might serve as an after-hours joint. In a single-story dwelling, a few rooms in front or back might suffice. Usually a basement was converted.[47] Food could be provided inexpensively from collard greens, smothered cabbage, beans or chittlins, which were often obtained free of charge. Cornbread, fried fish, pigs' feet, spaghetti, and that southern African-American delicacy, fried chicken, were standard fare.

The offerings in the after-hours joint, and even the physical setup of tables and music, had precursors in the illegal cabarets and buffet flats frequented by entertainers and Pullman porters.[48] Buffet flats, or "good-time flats," were privately owned establishments in apartments or houses and featured gambling and erotic shows, or what later came to be called "shake dancers." The term *buffet* was applied because these places had a variety of offerings, sometimes including drugs and homosexual encounters. Bessie Smith apparently was a devotee of buffet flats. These clubs had a reputation for being secure from violence; thefts were rare. They were originally set up for entertainers and Pullman porters whose contacts, gentlemanly manners, and good incomes gained them respect in black communities.

Most of the early after-hours clubs in New York were run and patronized by African-Americans. One such hangout was Ike Hines', a basement spot that opened in 1883. Hines was a former entertainer with the Hicks and Sawyers Georgia Minstrels; he also played banjo in the Billy Kersands sextette, a minstrel-era group that did the walkaround and an old-style plantation cakewalk. This experience undoubtedly exposed Hines to the southern jook tradition. Ike's originally catered only to performers and neighborhood folks, but anyone who could dance, sing, or play an instrument was always welcome. Located near Minetta Lane and Third Street, Ike's place soon became the liveliest joint in Greenwich Village, then a community with a high black concentration. In 1890s the club relocated to West 53rd Street and continued catering to the African-American performer and members of the sporting elite.[49]

These buffet flats and entertainers' hangouts gradually became alternatives to white clubs that did not admit African-Americans. Later, especially in the urban North, they evolved into after-hours joints that served the general black community. The competitive musicianship known as "cutting contests" that later became popular in Harlem's rent parties actually went on much earlier in these underground clubs. This competition can be viewed as a survival of an African tradition in African-American culture. Like its precursors the classic jook and the honky-tonk, the after-hours joint reflected the changing meaning of work for African-Americans. In the world of the jook, work existed in an economy of subsistence, of informal bondage shared by sharecroppers and agricultural laborers. Success meant getting the crop in without being in debt the next year. In the jook gambling was frequently done out of need, not sport as in after-hours joints or honky-tonks, where success was expressed in consumption, entertainment, and sporting activity. Terms such as "good time," "sweet man," "sporty," "jelly roll," and others attest to the relative extravagance of this new lifestyle. But even after black night clubs, legal cabarets, and membership clubs became common, after-hours joints flourished.

The after-hours joint, like the street lottery known as the numbers, became an important element in the underground business structure of black America. Almost anyone could open a business. Outside forces, such as organized crime or politicians, had little interest in them. Only occasionally, when an operation became too profitable or well known, was it forced into an encounter with the police. In the urban North, politicians would offer "protection" in exchange for votes. This kind of relationship would become routine as new dance and culture arenas emerged. [50]

In rural jooks and honky-tonks, particularly those located in or around labor camps, order was ultimately maintained by the white quarterboss or his delegate, a situation not much different from that under slavery.

Elsewhere, a variety of methods to maintain order was used. In extreme instances, the police were called, sometimes too late to prevent a killing. Some after-hours joint operators required patrons to check their weapons upon entering the premises.[51] This was a wise business practice, since killings could ruin the reputation of an otherwise successful enterprise. Usually the sponsor was responsible for keeping order:

> Poppa Jazz moved constantly serving whiskey, talking to visitors in the blues room, and leaning out its side door to encourage groups in the parking lot to come in. Occasionally he danced alone or performed a toast in front of Thomas, then resumed selling whiskey. Jazz knew his customers well, and those prone to fighting were closely watched and asked to leave if they became too loud. After escorting a man out the door he turned to me and said, "That was a bad one. They tell me a woman shot his nuts off in Chicago."[52]

More sophisticated places hired the services of a bouncer, but if no bouncer was present, patrons usually intervened once disputes progressed beyond a certain point.

The movement from jook to honky-tonk to after-hours joint was paralleled by changes in dances and music, even though the dances were often called by the same name or appeared very similar in movement. Differences in lifestyle had an effect. Painstaking hairdos—particularly women's if professionally fashioned with a pressing comb and hot curlers (rather than by oneself or friends)—limited the amount of perspiration dancers were willing to work up. Excessive effort could ruin a freshly hot-combed hairdo, a matter of real concern to the sophisticated after-hours patron.

Dances became more upright and less flat-footed, with fewer agrarian references, subtle changes that indicate a movement away from agricultural labor. As dance became more associated with sexuality and the free consumption of pleasure, the partnering relationship, which in the jook still had some communal ties to group dancing, became more isolated and individualized. The "sport" and the "good-time gal" were people of the moment. Hip shaking and pelvic innuendo were now more of a statement to one's partner than to one's community, except as executed by dancers in entertainers' hangouts or when all attention turned to one performer.

Between 1877 and 1920, African-Americans saw their music and dance adopted (poorly) by the white theater, the recording industry, and the newly emerging popular culture industry, while they suffered systematic exclusion from those markets. The songs of Mae West, Sophie Tucker, and Tin Pan Alley, Ann Pennington's black bottom, and the dances of Vernon and Irene Castle transformed black culture into something that white Americans could safely partake of. They led to the white invasion of black cabarets and the outright exploitive commercialization of African-American entertainment of the next three decades. Still, though tidied up and rendered bland, African-American dance and music permeated American households as never before. In this way the black and white cultures merged to form a distinct entity on the western international scene.

The classic jook did not survive the urban environment except as a descriptive term. Its transformation into the honky-tonk and after-hours joint parallels the evolution of rural farm labor into the urban proletariat. Yet, the jook manifested itself in still another institution, the rent party. Like its predecessors, the rent party offered dancing, drinking, food, and gambling. The essential difference was that the rent party, the most recent development on the jook continuum, was a transient, not a permanent, establishment.

Rent Parties, Chittlin' Struts, Blue Monday Affairs

Between 1900 and 1920 more than one million African-Americans poured into urban industrial centers like New York, Chicago, Detroit, Philadelphia, Buffalo, and Cleveland. Southern black migrants were but one component in a major shift of population into industrializing cities. The unprecedented demand for housing far outstripped availability, particularly in the areas relegated to blacks in the informal segregation that prevailed in the North. Overcrowded neighborhoods, exorbitant house prices and rents, and greedy absentee landlords provided the setting in which the rent party flourished. Rent parties were given to raise money. By 1920 rent parties—known variously as chittlin' struts, blue Monday affairs, house shouts, and too-bad parties, among others—were a common feature of black community life.[53]

Landlords perceived the influx of migrants as a major opportunity to cash in on even the most run-down properties. They began to convert one-family homes into multiple dwelling units, crowding as many people as possible into one house. Multiroom apartments became single-room "kitchenettes," with kitchen equipment installed in a clothes closet. In this way suites that formerly brought in $20 per month could yield $60 or more. Kitchenettes were inadequate as housing, but still better than the attics, basements, hallways, and closets rented for "sleeping rooms."[54]

Although their industrial jobs paid African-American workers relatively good wages (but generally lower than white workers' wages), high rents took a disproportionate amount when their rents and incomes are compared with those of white families. Cleveland's situation is a good example of the conditions that prevailed in many cities. African-American families were being charged 38 percent more rent than their white counterparts, for poorer housing. Blacks usually shared their unit with several other families, and paid for it from an income about one-third lower than that of comparable white families. In other words, the white family was paying 20 percent of its annual income for rent, while the black family was paying 34 percent for vastly inferior accommodations. Furthermore, the low level of owner occupancy left the community open to the exploitation of landlords. Absentee landlords, who rented out substandard housing but lived elsewhere, made handsome profits on properties they allowed to deteriorate, knowing that the tenants were virtually trapped. In 1940 only 10.1 percent of the dwellings in the Central area of Cleveland were owner occupied; 90 percent of all families in the Central area were renting, and comparable areas in New York and Chicago were not much different.[55]

The pressure of the monthly rent bill was especially strong on African-Americans. Their remedy: traditional cultural resources, here in the form of the rent
party. The rent party stems from two divergent traditions: the jook and the church social, the latter a Sunday outing that included music and the sale of box
lunches or dinners, usually to raise money for the
church or to pay the minister's salary. Both flourished
in the South before migration.

> For many years it has been the custom of certain
> portions of the Negro group living in Southern
> cities to give some form of a party when money was
> needed to supplement the family income. The pur-
> pose for giving such a party was never stated, but
> who cared whether the increment was used to pay
> the next installment on the "Steinway" or the week-
> ly rent?[56]

With migrations, both traditions began growing on
the northern urban scene. Deplorable living conditions proved fertile ground not only for the necessity of
the rent party, but for its further development. Established northern neighbors were not receptive to this
solution, though they well understood the problem:

> With the mass movement of Southern Negroes to
> Northern cities came their little custom. Harlem
> was astounded. Socially minded individuals
> claimed that . . . the relative insufficiency of
> wages was entirely responsible for this ignominious
> situation; that the exorbitant rents paid by the
> Negro wage earners had given the rise to the
> obnoxious "house rent party." The truth seems to
> be that the old party of the South had attired itself à

la Harlem. Within a few years the custom developed into a business venture whereby a tenant sought to pay a rent four, five, and six times as great as was paid in the South. It developed by-products both legal and otherwise, hence it became extremely popular.[57]

According to George Gould, a performer who assisted at rent parties, "the rent party originated the first time a black person had to pay his rent and couldn't." Gould remembers rent parties as early as a few years after World War I, when he was a youngster. They became much more frequent after the onset of the Depression when the rates of African-American unemployment soared. Semiskilled industrial work was frequently recognized as a dead end. An occupational color line prevented blacks from acquiring greater skills, and they were systematically excluded from apprenticeships and training programs. In Cleveland's black neighborhoods, unemployment ranged from 50 to 90 percent.[58]

With economic resources at an all-time low, many African-Americans turned to the rent party as an alternative to both commercial entertainment and employment. The rent party provided entertainment and fellowship while enabling the sponsor to pay the rent and cover a few other expenses. Had a political organization or strong tenants' movement addressed housing needs, the rent party might not have developed such support. However, with practically no political power and virtually no economic clout, African-Americans had few options. Other coping strategies, such as gambling or prostitution, were problematic and gambling was dominated by men. The house rent party, on the other hand, could be carried off successfully by either men or women in their own homes with the approval of the community.[59]

The rent shout, as they were also known, was a transient after-hours joint, a temporary jook. Sponsoring one required little more than a place to hold it. One's own dwelling was the usual choice, but if inadequate, then the dwelling of a friend, who thereby became a cosponsor. It featured dancing, music, food, liquor, and some type of gambling. How did impoverished individuals manage to sponsor such a variety of activities? By establishing a cooperative network, a core of other individuals willing to assist. Usually a promise to return the courtesy was sufficient. This volunteer work was an investment against future hard times.[60]

The gambling at a rent shout usually involved cards or dice. According to hoofer Earl Royster, who helped run the gambling at his mother's regular rent shouts, usually a sheet or blanket was laid down to provide a surface. The person in charge was allowed to "cut," or take a percentage of all bets, usually 4 to 10 percent; or the sponsor agreed to pay the game operator a specific sum in advance. The gambling was usually physically separated from the other activities; if not in another room, it was a partitioned off, perhaps by a sheet flung across a clothesline.[61] Advance information that gambling would be featured guaranteed a certain constituency and assured the sponsors some cash return. Gambling, like dancing, required no initial outlay of scarce funds and returned a clear profit.

Liquor, essential at the successful rent shout, was sold to patrons; this practice, like gambling, was ille-

African-American dances were often policed. All photos courtesy of the Library of Congress, unless otherwise credited.

"Cut his mouth out, mamma."

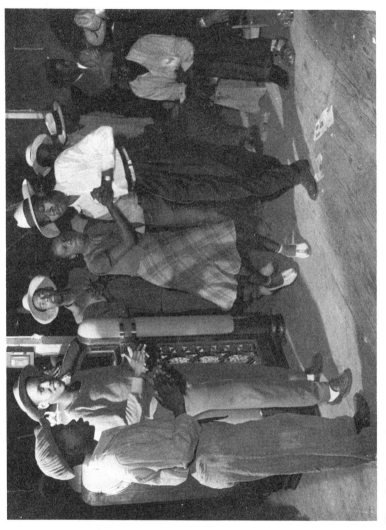

The jukebox transformed the interactive relationship between the dancer and the musician.

Elite balls such as these raised funds for a variety of causes.

Semiurban cafés such as these served as places where the urban strains of African-American cultural life met the rural.

Situated in rural areas, jooks like this provided live music, food, and dancing.

Jooking occurred on the plantation both openly and surreptitiously.

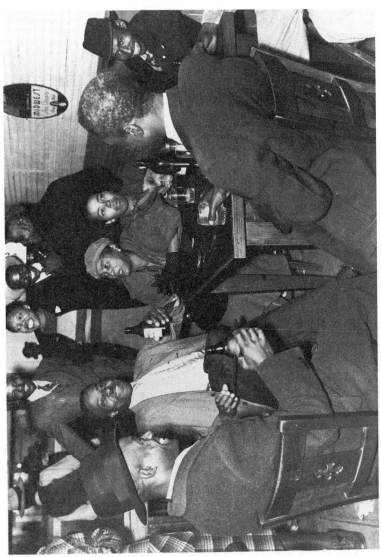

Membership clubs provided their patrons with some degree of privacy and freedom from racial harrassment.

Membership club.

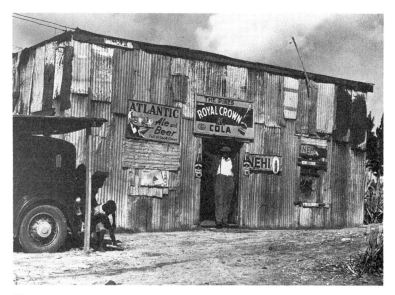

The classic jook.

Membership clubs used placards such as these to advertise their upcoming affairs.

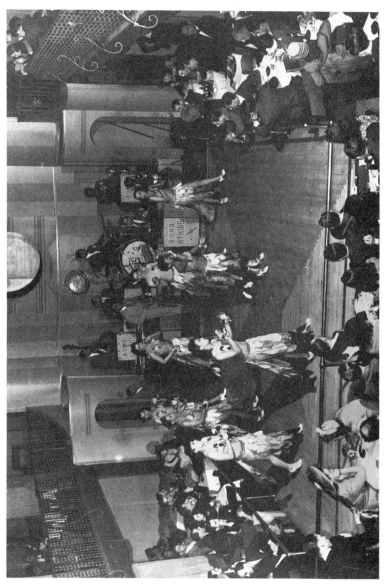

Chicago "black and tan" cabaret.

Children observed jook-house dances.

Contemporary elite balls continue longstanding traditions. John Mosley Photographer/Charles L. Blockson Afro-American Collection, Temple University.

gal. Nevertheless, alcohol could be purchased either legally or from a neighborhood bootlegger (or manufactured by the sponsor). If funds were low, a bootlegger might be invited to sell liquor himself, with a percentage going to the sponsor. The person in charge of liquor sales would construct a makeshift bar. Articles as unpretentious as two old washtubs and a wooden slat board with a sheet draped across could serve the purpose, although arrangements could be far more elaborate. During Prohibition, the liquor was often kept in the kitchen, sold there, and dispensed from a coffee pot; when requesting a drink, one would merely ask for a cup of coffee.[62]

Music was generally furnished by a musician on a piano or guitar. According to interviews I conducted, the musician would usually play for a good meal and all the liquor he could drink. Apparently musicians considered the "rent shout circuit" an excellent arena in which to hone their skills. Stiff competition, referred to as "cutting contests," were common; one musician after another would take his turn demonstrating his skill. This practice spilled over from the honky-tonks, jooks, and after-hours joints, but its roots go back to Africa, where such competitions are still common. The famous Harlem rent parties provided apprenticeship for musicians like Fats Waller, Willie (the Lion) Smith, Duke Ellington, Eubie Blake, and James P. Johnson.[63]

Musicians had the power to make or break these functions. They interacted with the patrons and created an atmosphere of fellowship and frivolity. Author Wallace Thurman describes a rent party musician at work:

When they returned to the room, the pianist was just preparing to play again. He was tall and slender with extra long legs and arms, giving him the appearance of a scarecrow. His pants were tight in the waist and full in the legs. He wore no coat, and a blue silk shirt hung damply to his body. He acted as if he were king of the occasion, ruling all from his piano stool throne. He talked familiarly to every one in the room, called women from other men's arms, demanded drinks from any bottle he happened to see being passed around, laughed uproariously, and made many grotesque and ofttimes obscene gestures. [64]

If musicians were unavailable, prerecorded music in the form of a Victrola, piano roll, or radio provided substitutes. When the jukebox appeared in black communities in the late 1920s and early 1930s, it provided an additional means of making money. Some rent parties had jukeboxes temporarily installed for the occasion. A jukebox could be leased for any period of time, no matter how short. The company would set up a box for a flat fee. If the sponsors lacked funds a commission agreement could be worked out. These could be very liberal, with the company taking as little as 10 percent of the profits. The lenience in lease and rental resulted because the jukeboxes could not begin to compete with the attraction of live musicians. Sometimes the machines were installed for nothing in an effort to develop the taste of consumers, but they were not fully accepted until the late 1940s or early 1950s. By that time rent parties had died out and the nature of music production and black entertainment had changed. [65]

The bill of fare at these occasions was generally less elaborate than at after-hours joints, since food and liquor required an outlay of cash. Food could be obtained in several ways. Chittlins were frequently served at rent parties (thus the name chittlin' strut); these hog intestines were often discarded by the local meatpacking houses, given away, or sold for the cost of the material they were packed in. People commonly asked workers on the loading docks to save the chittlins for them. They may have been free, but chittlins were not easy to prepare. Unlike today's frozen chittlins, those from the loading docks came packed in salt; they had to be split and the salt and the contents washed out. Then they were carefully cleaned by the older children in the household. Other food items could be acquired cheaply or with the promise of favors. Cabbage or chicken might come from neighbors, since small livestock and vegetable gardens were kept in many black communities, particularly by migrants from the South. Other foods included "hoppin' john" (blackeye peas and rice), mulatto rice (rice and tomatoes), sweet potato or corn pone, gumbo, collard greens, pigs' feet, and hog maws. The menu varied according to availability and the region from which the migrants came.[66]

Once the logistics of music, location, gambling, food, and liquor were settled, the affair had only to advertise. News spread quickly through the densely populated black communities of the urban North, primarily by word of mouth. Even when hand-printed tickets were passed out or sold in advance, the grapevine drew the majority of participants.[67] But tickets were printed anyway, if only to verify a paid admission.

Some tickets had rhymes on them, promising a night of raucous entertainment.

> Shake it, break it, Hang it on the wall
> sling it out the window and catch it before it falls.

> Save your tears for a rainy day,
> We are giving a party where you can play
> With red mammas and too bad Sheabas
> Who wear their dresses above their knees
> And mess around with whom they please.[68]

The use of printed tickets was probably most widespread in Harlem because of street printers who made them a speciality:

> There has been an evolution in the eclat of the rent party since it has become "Harlemized." No longer does the entrepreneur depend upon the music to simply welcome his stranger guests; nor does he simply invite friends of the neighborhood. There straggles along the cross-town streets of North Harlem a familiar figure the Wayside Printer, pushing a little cart which has all of the equipment necessary for setting up the rent party ticket. While you wait, he sets up your invitation with the ballyhoo heading desired, and at a very reasonable price. What work the Wayside Printer does not get goes to the nearest print shop; some of which specialize in these announcements.[69]

Tickets often guaranteed a larger party, but required a substantial outlay of cash. Numbers runners, who had a high degree of access to the black community, also advertised upcoming rent shouts. All one had to do was tell the local numbers runner and soon everyone on his route knew about it too.[70] And inevitably, the music and noise of a party in progress attracted additional patrons.

Wherever large numbers of African-Americans were living—Memphis, Chicago, Birmingham, New York, Detroit, St. Louis, Philadelphia, Cleveland—rent parties became established cultural institutions with their own regional variations. They were the product of cooperation, but remained essentially an individual response to a large-scale problem. They provided escape for some and an alternative to eviction for many, but they could not galvanize the community into a political unit. As the Depression worsened and large-scale evictions occurred, black protest increased, but to little effect. Resentment in Cleveland reached an exploding point in 1939 when black leaders threatened a rent strike. The threat was never realized; instead, a mayor's "fair rent committee" was appointed to study high rentals and violations of housing codes. But this committee (and others elsewhere) was incapable of handling the problem, and was further hampered by the escalating density fed by wartime migration. In Cleveland the committee dealt with complaints one by one, and in one two-week period adjusted only fifty cases.[71]

The process of ghettoization accelerated in the period between the wars. People were forced out of work and more families took in boarders, increasing community density even further. As housing in most urban areas worsened and unemployment reached an all-time high, the frequency of rent parties increased. When economic conditions improved somewhat after World War II, rent parties began to decline. Black-owned clubs flourished as never before, providing new entertainment options that undercut rent parties; also, post–World War II employment—limited as it was—eased the housing strain.

> The rent parties have not been so frequent of late. Harlem's new dance halls with their lavish entertainment, double orchestra and their "sixteen hours of continuous dancing," with easy chairs and refreshments available are ruining the business. They who continue in this venture of pleasure and business are working on a very close margin both socially and economically. [72]

Rent parties provided an even more intimate arena for dancing than the jooks or after-hours joints. Expressions such as "dancin' on a dime" testify to their density. The dances themselves, like the cuisine, varied according to chronology and region. Most were southern imports; they included the Charleston and the black bottom, two old jook-house dances, and also the camel, the messaround, the shimmy, the skate, the sand, and the buzzard. [73] Some were identical to those performed in the South; others were variations or derivations. For example, the buzzard was probably an urbanized derivative of the buzzard lope. The camel, messaround, sand, and skate all produced variations that appeared in African-American communities in the late 1950s and early 1960s.

Like the music at the chittlin' strut, the dancing occasionally turned to rivalries, known also as "cutting." One mark of a good dancer was the ability to embellish one's performance with as many vernacular steps as possible. Poet Maya Angelou describes how it is done:

He spoke to the other players, counted down four
and the music began. I started dancing, rushing
into movement, making up steps and changing direction. There was no story, no plan, I simply put
every dance I had ever seen or known into my body
and onto the stage. A little rhumba, tango, jitterbug, Susy-Q, trucking, snake hips, conga,
charleston and cha-cha. When the music was finished I had exhausted my repertoire and myself.[74]

Before the migration of the southern migrants, the
northern black elite had more visibility as the arbiter
of publicly displayed black culture. With each succes-
sive migrant wave, the culture of the southern working
classes came to be viewed by outsiders (and by itself)
as the dominant strain. In jooks and after-hours joints
and at rent shouts, dance became a litmus test for sociocultural identity. The old elite was not only a minority within a minority, it had also rejected public
display of core cultural forms for Euro-American ones.
While the elite continued to give formal dances, the
working classes were imprinting the southern regional dance and music deeper on the African-American
population. The black working class carefully and sen-
sitively guarded social dance as its province.[75] Before
long, the black elite recognized its inability to set the
standards for the non-elite community. In 1929 Wallace Thurman described this uneasy social division:

He had become acquainted with a young Negro
writer, who had asked him to escort a group of
young writers and artists to a house-rent party.
Though they had heard much of this phenomenon,
none had been on the inside of one, and because of
their rather polished manners and exteriors, were

afraid that they might not be admitted. Proletarian Negroes are as suspicious of their more sophisticated brethren as they are of white men, and resent as keenly their intrusion into their social world.[76]

Imbued with a deep sense of obligation for racial uplift, which for immigrants of all kinds has often meant leaving the past behind, the black elite is at pains to deny its alienation from core black culture. Ralph Ellison provides an illustration. Responding to charges that black intellectuals have deserted core black culture, he states: "Part of my pride in being what I am is that as a dancer, as a physical man . . . I bet you I can outdance, outrif most of those intellectuals who're supposed to have come back." Note that Ellison asserts that his dancing ability clears him of the charge—but he essentially confirms the guilt of others. In his autobiography, Malcolm X describes his prowess—and misspent time—as a jitterbug dancer, recognizing Euro-American cultural domination as a root of division between the black elite and the working classes: "Whites are correct in thinking that black people are natural dancers. Even little kids are—except for those Negroes today who are so 'integrated' as I had been, that their instincts are inhibited."[77]

Working-class blacks frequently use the term *integrated* to disparage African-Americans who do not exhibit what they consider "black" behavior. What Malcolm refers to as "instinct" is not biological, but rather the results of exposure to black working-class experiences at home and in the neighborhood. Few of today's children have seen a rent party; these seem to have disappeared, at least in their traditional form. In the late 1960s and early 1970s "pay parties" appeared in several locales, but there are significant differences: the patrons are younger, much less needy; admission is charged at the door and recorded music is used exclusively. Still, even in adapted forms rent shouts remain a viable source for quickly raising funds.

3

UPPER SHADIES AND URBAN POLITICS

"They used the social activity to corral the black vote!"
— Charles Carr, black politician

Monday Night at the Paradise Ballroom

CAUGHT between the traditions of the past and new experiences in cities, blacks evolved into a social life that eventually became enmeshed in commercial urban entertainments. The transition was not easy. The jook and its derivative forms served a vital cultural function, but African-Americans readily saw how restricted their social opportunities were compared with those of whites: "See, back then it was different, blacks had no place to go except to what you call after-hours places. Back then the white folks wouldn't allow us to go nowhere. Now things have opened up."[1]

The jook in any of its forms could spring up anywhere in the black community. Practically all that was necessary was the desire to make it happen; community members themselves controlled the necessary resources. Dance halls, membership clubs, night clubs, and block parties, on the other hand, all required the cooperation of local public officials. These new entertainments were products of the modern urban environment—indeed, a response to it—and it was inevitable that the recent migrants as well as upwardly mobile African-Americans would move to experience them.

The urban North was vastly more complex than the rural environment that produced the jook and the jook-house dances. First, the lifestyle, work rhythms, and types of employment were more sophisticated and varied. Migrants who had previously spent their leisure hours fishing, attending church, telling folk tales, or enjoying the jooks found themselves confronted with new commercial offerings and the extra money to pay for them.[2] And, since they no longer worked from sunup to sundown, they had more time to spend their surplus cash.

As the urban experience gradually redefined the sense of community and self, it similarly affected the content and execution of the dances. Like other institutions, the dances began gradually relinquishing their rural character. For example, the southern dance step called milking the cow involved flat-footed rocking of the hips from side to side, with knees bent as if seated on a milking stool, and hands moving as if actually milking a cow. This same hip—foot coordination appeared in the northern Midwest in the 1950s as a dance embellishment known as the toilet stool. It reappeared in the 1960s as the base of movements in the Watusi. Its most recent revival was in the late 1970s as the rock. The snake hips, a dance found on southern plantations before emancipation, demonstrates a similar evolution. It was popularized in Harlem in the 1920s by Earl "Snake Hips" Tucker.[3] It emerged in the late 1950s as poppin' the hips and in the early 1980s as the pop. In the 1950s the movement was used primarily as an embellishment rather than as a dance itself. It was designed to "burn," or outdance, one's partner or opponent, but in both the earlier and later periods it existed as an independent dance in its own right.

The cramped living conditions in northern cities, though accommodating to a rent party or small affair, encouraged people to seek entertainment outside the home. But where could they go? The racist atmosphere in northern cities intensified as the number of African-American migrants increased. Before the migration, downtown businesses were generally open to anyone who could pay their price. This policy tolerated a few members of the old black elite, although simple economics excluded the vast majority of African-Americans. As urban blacks swelled in number, however, toleration turned to exclusion. Many businesses openly refused to serve African-Americans, theaters segregated them in balconies, and hotels refused them accommodations. Public amusement parks would not permit African-Americans in their dance halls or swimming pools. In most cities both the YMCA and the YWCA instituted "whites-only" policies by 1915.[4] Faced with racial discrimination abetted by poverty, African-Americans were compelled to create additional opportunities for recreation within their own communities.

Unlike the jooks, which were independently operated, block parties, membership clubs, night clubs, and dance halls were intertwined in the commercial and political fabric of city life; they made money for a considerable number of people, and involved a range of officials, from building inspectors to representatives of the mayor's office. They could grant permission and licenses as they pleased. Average citizens without capital or political clout were in no position to open establishments of this sort. Political power had become a determinant.

The new black dance arenas had analoges in the white community, but their respective institutions would never be mistaken for each other. The jook continuum imparted a distinct identity to the new forms. Rent parties, honky-tonks, after-hours joints, membership clubs, dance halls, and night clubs existed simultaneously and cross fertilized each other, forming a conglomerate of black working-class cultural institutions.

American public dance halls originated in the nineteenth-century concert saloon, which first appeared in urban areas in the 1840s and 1850s and reached a peak in popularity between 1880 and 1910. Saloon dance halls were widespread in cities like San Francisco, which in 1910 had more than 300 within a six-block area; Chicago's South Side had 285. In 1911 Louise deKoven Bowen of Chicago's Juvenile Protection Association reported 306 licensed and about 100 unlicensed public dance halls in Chicago. A survey in Cleveland in 1911 showed 130 dance halls, 56 of them connected to establishments selling liquor and 39 actually located over saloons. Other forms of public dancing were available. Russel Nye distinguishes five types: dances sponsored by social work agencies, particularly those concerned with juveniles; club dances, lodge dances, and charity balls; public dancing at hotels; taxi dance halls; and "dance palaces," which might be located at an amusement park or outdoor pavilion. All five appeared in most northern urban areas. [5]

The potent racist atmosphere makes it no surprise that the color barrier was rigidly enforced at dance halls. None of the public halls in Cleveland, for example, including those in amusement and city parks, would admit African-Americans on an equal basis with whites. Euclid Beach Park, a local amusement facility, never admitted African-Americans to the dance hall; it excluded blacks from the day it opened until the day it closed. Articles in the black press complained about its segregationist practices as early as 1899, and publicized a number of suits filed against Euclid Beach. In the 1940s a city councilmember succeeded in pushing through an ordinance that mandated the loss of license for racial discrimination in dance halls, but it was largely ignored. As late as 1946 incidents of police brutality, assaults, and arrests were still common results of the "whites-only" restriction. Luna Park, a similar facility, eventually allowed African-Americans to use the dance hall on a segregated basis. Before World War II, however, articles in the local black weekly, *The Gazette,* complained regularly about segregation in Luna Park's dance hall and swimming pool areas. [6]

Most dance halls in Cleveland eventually adopted a policy of admitting African-Americans one night a week, usually on Mondays. Black groups or clubs would rent the hall for a set fee and charge their patrons admission; this allowed a club to make a few dollars. The rule of "one night only" was apparently acceptable to whites and was adopted by both private and municipal dance facilities. According to people I interviewed, including a city councilmember who helped pass an antidiscrimination ordinance, segregation of the races was the policy enforced by dance halls in Cleveland until after World War II.[7]

Cleveland was not the only city frightened by the specter of integrated dancing. The Savoy Ballroom memorialized, in the popular tune "Stompin' at the Savoy," was one of Harlem's best-known cultural showcases. Located at Lenox Avenue and 140th Street, owned by Moe Gale and managed by Charles Buchanon, the Savoy brought nationally famous musicians such as Cab Calloway and Louis Armstrong together with talented local dancers and patrons from all races and classes. For nearly twenty years musicians and dancers of all backgrounds frequented the ballroom. It employed ninety persons on an annual payroll of $150,000 and also served as a rental hall for community clubs and organizations sponsoring benefits. But its truly integrated atmosphere generated much attention, particularly among the police who expressed concern about interracial dancing. Citizens wrote letters to the mayor rallying against "miscegenation," "white whores" and "niggers" in the integrated ballroom and pleading for an end to such activity.[8]

On March 24, 1943, the dance-hall license of the Savoy was revoked in an attempt to keep whites out of Harlem. Though prostitutes working out of the Savoy were given as the official reason, a black journalist speculated that white dance-hall owners and downtown businessmen had sought the closing in order to monopolize white patrons. In all probability an alliance that included the police, the white dance-hall establishment, and the general public pushed for and welcomed the Savoy's demise.[9] Even in Harlem, as across the nation, African-American urban dwellers suffered from restricted access to public dance facilities.

Church groups sometimes rented halls and sponsored dances, but most dances advertised in the black press were given by private clubs. Organizations such as the black Elks club arranged dances to celebrate holidays or events such as the installation of newly elected officers, and practically every issue of the *Cleveland Gazette* carried ads for private affairs.[10] The Caterers Club, formed in 1903 by George Myers and several other "old Cleveland" blacks, was composed primarily of barbers, waiters, and caterers, the elite of Negro society; it gave an annual ball and banquet in a rented facility outside the black community.[11]

Most of the formal and semiformal affairs took place at white-owned halls, and so the sponsors relinquished some control over the event. Most could not be held during the customary leisure hours of the weekend, because prime time was reserved for white use. At sites like Woodluff Hall, located in Cleveland's heavily black Central Avenue district, dances could be held on any night, but dance halls that served the black community were often viewed as disreputable by both blacks and whites. Some perceived the very presence of dance halls to be a problem. There was general concern over Woodluff Hall, political strongman Albert

"Starlight" Boyd's dance hall. Jane Edna Hunter, who arrived in Cleveland in 1905, explains why:

> One evening loneliness and desire for a little fun—I had had no recreation since coming to Cleveland—lead me to accept an invitation to go to Woodluff Hall. There would be good dancing and good music, I was told. True enough, the music was good. But there was not a little in the conduct and appearance of the guests to cause me uneasiness—women with heavily painted faces and indecently short skirts; men slightly intoxicated and somewhat noisy. I learned late that there was a saloon on the first floor, but enlightenment came only by a happy chance. A neatly dressed young man introduced himself and asked me to dance. After the dance he tarried for a few minutes conversation. I gave him my name, my profession and told him how I was earning and hoped to continue to earn a living in Cleveland. "Little girl," he said, looking seriously at me and speaking somewhat severely, "you're in the wrong church and the wrong pew. This is not the place for nice girls like you. I want you to meet my mother and sister." Woodluff Hall, I discovered was the resort of bad women, coming largely from the Hamilton Avenue district. It was also a recruiting station for the notorious "Starlight"—procurer for wild, wealthy, men. [12]

The general movement against dance halls that surfaced around the turn of the century had proponents in the black community as well. A reform movement sprung up in Cleveland in 1908, but was short-lived. From 1910 to 1912 the Anti-Saloon League, composed primarily of clergymen, campaigned vigorously against liquor sales, saloons, and dance halls.

They addressed black audiences directly through their churches, and their campaign was buttressed when a shooting in the Wilson and Brown saloon left one Walter Jackson dead. Black leaders called meetings to protest the lack of police protection in their community. A committee met with Mayor Newton D. Baker, who consented to crack down on saloon-style dance halls. A new ordinance installed a dance-hall inspector, required licensing for the halls, and imposed a curfew on dances. Thus encouraged, the reformers engaged in shutting down some thirty-two "cheap neighborhood saloon halls" because "the building or their surrounding conditions were such as to render them unfit for dance halls."[13] Unfit or not, these closings tightened the pinch on the black community's recreational outlets.

Saloon dance halls were important centers for community contacts as well as for recreation. Like saloons in white ethnic communities, they reinforced ethnic and class ties. On the one hand black dance halls encouraged assimilation because they required conformity to public social standards. On the other hand they deterred assimilation because they reinforced core culture class and ethnic ties.[14] After they closed, no other institutions quite replaced them. Although jooks, after-hours joints, and even rent parties did so to a degree, only with the emergence of night clubs did a social arena fully express black ambivalence toward cultural assimilation.

Dance demonstrates the ambivalence perfectly. African-Americans consistently brought new forms involving African movement motifs to America's dance halls. The turkey trot, the foxtrot, and the monkey glide are a few of the dances popular in early twentieth-century dance halls. The turkey trot in particular caused an uproar. According to Stearns, it "consisted of a fast marching one-step, arms pumping at the side, with occasional arms-flapping emulating a crazed turkey."[15] The "inappropriate" movements developed in the jooks where upper-class notions of respectability had little power.

Closing the saloon dance halls in Cleveland proved a real immediate hardship for the black community. It almost exterminated the public dance life of those living in congested sections of the city, according to Robert O. Bartholomew, the city's dance-hall inspector. Cleveland was a model for other cities in dance-hall legislation. The city inaugurated a municipal dance hall as early as 1912, but that did not remedy a growing problem, which was exacerbated by the high rental cost of the remaining halls. The public halls cost from $25 to $50 more than the older, cheaper halls, way beyond the reach of the average citizen. Nor did closing the dance saloons have much effect in eliminating vice. Within a few years the ordinance governing dance halls was largely ignored; musicians resented a cutback in their employment and exerted pressure that made enforcement difficult.[16]

The alliances of Cleveland's newly elected black twelfth-ward councilman-at-large, Thomas Fleming, prevented him from campaigning against vice, even if he had been inclined to do so. Fleming had been associated with Republican party politics before World War I. In 1904 he had been elected a delegate to the party convention that nominated Theodore Roosevelt. By 1907 he was running for public office as part of the

Republican machine. During Fleming's early political career he became associated with Albert D. Boyd, owner of taverns, real estate, and dance halls. Boyd's hostelry at East 14th and Scovil Avenue became the center of Republican eleventh-ward politics. (Due to redistricting, the eleventh and twelfth wards represent the same neighborhoods.) Prominent in real estate through acts of charity to needy families, through his taverns and dance hall, Woodluff Hall, Albert Boyd controlled and manipulated the black vote in the most heavily Republican ward in the city. "Starlight" Boyd was Fleming's biggest patron.[17]

The *Gazette* frequently editorialized against this politician–businessman alliance, an arrangement that allowed "speakeasies," "gambling halls," and other vice in the Central area because of "police protection" provided by the local councilman. "Not satisfied, it seems, with a saloon, the Douglass 'Club' and the Ideal Hall dancing 'school' he would also have a grill. Is there anything else 'Star' and Tom want?" In another editorial, the *Gazette* complained, "It is said that 'Star,' Tom and 'Germany' are running dances at Ideal (Woodluff) Hall. The 'boys' are wanting to know if there is anything else they want. It looks as if someone is trying to break up the Teutonia Hall Dances."[18]

In an attempt to neutralize the attraction of Woodluff Hall and other dance halls like it, the supervisor of school extension began a series of weekly social gatherings at the local high school. In Cleveland, the debate over the use of local school auditoriums for dances began as early as 1912; similar discussions occurred in other cities. The demand for respectable recreation was so strong that, according to Julia

Schoenfeld, field secretary of the Playground and Recreation Association, factories in some cities opened recreation rooms and began conducting dances. Churches joined the effort to provide more respectable amusement. The *Gazette* carried ads for dances sponsored by various church clubs, and between 1900 and 1920 the number of newspaper ads for church-sponsored dances increased noticeably. Jane Edna Hunter, founder of the Phillis Wheatley Association, saw the inauguration of a Phillis Wheatley recreation hall as the solution to the "evil influence which the commercial dance hall was exerting upon the morals of the Negroes."[19] The association rented a barn, put in a new floor, and plastered the walls. It charged admission for the dances and parties it gave twice a month, but guests were admitted on invitation only, so this endeavor had no hope of reaching masses who frequented the saloon dance halls.

Other than the dance halls that served the black community, options for public dancing were few. The dances sponsored by private clubs reached only an audience that perceived itself as upwardly mobile. Organizations like the Phillis Wheatley Association gave dances for teenagers and high school students in every major city. White-owned dance halls continued their "whites-only" policy, allowing African-Americans the customary one night per week. On that night black promoters brought in live music of all types, including famous big bands. Police security was beefed up for these occasions. Many white-owned dance halls employed a house band, but these rarely suited African-American tastes. These Monday night affairs were generally larger and the admission more costly than for white dances. Unlike the jooks, they involved participation in ritualized aspects of black culture on a mass scale. Dancing assumed a new importance. Malcolm X provides an example from Boston:

Now Count Basie turned on the showtime blast, and the other dancers moved off the floor, shifting for good watching positions, and began their hollering for their favorites . . . the Count's band was wailing. I grabbed Mamie and we started to work. . . . I remember the very night that she became known as one of the showtime favorites there at the Roseland . . . she got barefoot and shouted and shook herself as if she were in some African jungle frenzy, and then she let loose with some dancing, shouting with every step. . . . The crowd loved any way-out lindying style that made a colorful show like that. It was how Mamie had become known.[20]

Crowds up to 1,200 people would pack a ballroom to dance to the sounds of well-known bands. The dances had their origin in the jook houses of five decades earlier, but in this new format they were shaped to a contemporary esthetic. The 1930s and 1940s, for example, saw the lindy hop at its peak of popularity. The dance halls allowed lindy hoppers significantly more room than did rent parties or after-hours joints, and lindying became more acrobatic. According to Langston Hughes, "The Lindy-hoppers at the Savoy even began to practice acrobatic routines, and to do absurd things for the entertainment of the whites, that probably never would have entered their heads to attempt merely for their own effortless amusement."[21]

On one level these dances can be seen as ironic analogs to the large public dances of urban slaves. Both activities cut across class lines, attracting lower-class, working-class, and some elite African-Americans. They provided an opportunity for cultural exchange unavailable in almost any other format.

The Universal Negro Improvement Association (UNIA) in Cleveland attempted to provide the overcrowded black community with a dance-hall facility. According to patrons, the UNIA gave dances in its attic. "They fixed up this attic, they had dark lights and they would get a small band."[22] Admission was twenty-five cents, and the dance lasted from eight o'clock until midnight. These dances attracted the working and lower classes and reached out to southern migrants in ways that other dances couldn't. But they were destined to extinction. They grew more popular between early 1930s and World War II, but after that they faded as blacks found better jobs and moved to other areas of the city.

In most cities politicians were more successful than churches, civic groups, and educational officials in establishing an alternative to dance halls. The general pattern in most urban areas was to exchange political favors for votes. Politicians not only inaugurated the first dance halls in many black communities, but used them for their own purposes. This system of patronage became a way to provide blacks with saloons, dance halls, and, as we shall see, membership clubs and night clubs.

Bells, Buzzers, an Air of Legitimacy

Membership clubs were privately sponsored social establishments that featured gambling, liquor, and food. The clubs that appeared in most northern urban black communities were sponsored by political groups (the Republican Club), by service or benevolent organizations (the Elks Club), or by a social group (the Twelve Counts). The earliest were backed by political parties.

Located on the outer edges of the black community at East 49th and Central Avenue, the first Republican Club in Cleveland opened its doors in 1903. It also served as a meeting place for the twelfth ward Republican organization. The spacious floor allowed it to double as a dance hall, and one of its back rooms served as a place for gambling. The second membership club, also under political sponsorship, was begun by a local politician and the first African-American elected to city council, Thomas Fleming. Fleming had been active in local Republican politics since the mid-1890s, when southern migration began to increase the black electorate. The pre–World War I migration, although small compared to what was to come later, was large enough to give African-Americans bargaining power on certain issues. The local Republicans had become accustomed to granting blacks a few concessions in exchange for their support.[23] They recognized the importance of the black vote and used black politicians to ensure it.

The earliest black politicians were not direct advocates for the black community in the way their successors would be. A larger black electorate meant that

leaders such as Fleming no longer had to depend totally on whites, but could use black voters as leverage in
garnering favors from Republican party leaders. Though
this pattern emerged earlier in larger cities, the first
influential alliance of this kind in Cleveland lay between Albert D. "Starlight" Boyd and Republican boss
Maurice Maschke.[24]

Born in rural Mississippi, Boyd was in his teens
when he journeyed to Cleveland to secure employment
in the 1880s. He soon allied himself with the local
Republican party. Ten years later, he purchased an establishment variously described as a saloon or tavern
or café (his connection with dance halls was mentioned earlier). Known as the Starlight Café, it soon
became the center of Republican activity in the eleventh ward. The growing black population gave Boyd
the incentive to secure its vote for the Republican party. He maintained control by "looking after the needs
of the people of his ward." He rented apartment buildings and houses to its occupants. In the absence of
organized charity, Starlight Boyd often sent food and
aid to the needy. The residents of his ward responded
by following his political advice, thus granting him
enormous control in the most heavily Republican
ward in the city.[25]

Boyd's popularity in the eleventh ward grew as he
expanded his real estate holdings, but his legitimate
business endeavors gradually gave way to increased
involvement in prostitution and gambling. According
to Jane Edna Hunter, the phenomenal growth rate of
the black community—300 percent increase between
1910 and 1920—made it susceptible to such exploi-

tation. The rural migrants provided easy pickings for unscrupulous politicians and landlords. [26]

Tom Fleming's ability to deliver the black vote in the increasingly black eleventh ward was in part the result of his association with Boyd. By 1905 the county branch of the Republican party acknowledged Fleming's growing political power by choosing him as ward leader and allowing him to dispense patronage. The first membership clubs were a result of that patronage. According to Charles Carr, who was active in Republican politics from the early 1920s, "Blacks had no place in the city; the white lodges and organizations had their private clubs." Political bargaining eventually resulted in the appearance of membership clubs in the black community of Cleveland. The first three establishments—the Z Douglass Club, the first "privately" sponsored club for African-Americans, begun by Boyd, the Starlight Café, and the Republican Club—originated as a result of political favors garnered from the party. [27]

It was less complicated to obtain a liquor permit for a membership club than for sale to the general public; it was also less expensive: $100, rather than $1,000 for a public license. However, even the less restrictive license was beyond the reach of most African-Americans. The private clubs gave the city's newly emerging black urban constituency a place to drink, dance, and otherwise be entertained. They also contained black social life within the confines of the nascent ghetto and prevented black establishments from attracting a significant white clientele. The setup apparently satisfied everyone.

The membership clubs were hardly the bastions of elite respectability that white gentlemen's clubs were. W. E. B. Du Bois, in his classic sociological study *The Philadelphia Negro,* draws a harsh portrait of the turn-of-the-century clubs in Philadelphia's black community:

> The loafers who line the curbs in these places are no fools, but sharp, wily men who often outwit both the Police Department and the Department of Charities. Their nucleus consists of a class of professional criminals, who do not work, figure in the rogues galleries of a half dozen cities, and migrate here and there. About these are a set of gamblers and sharpers who seldom are caught in serious crimes, but who nevertheless live from its proceeds and aid and abet it. The headquarters of all these are usually the political clubs and poolrooms; they stand ready to entrap the unwary and tempt the weak. [28]

The official name of Cleveland's earliest membership club was the Twelfth Ward Republican Club; its purpose, as stated by its founder, was to "combine and solidify the Afro-American voters." It sold liquor, ostensibly to its membership only, until Prohibition. Even then, according to a patron who recalled obtaining liquor at the club in 1922, "liquor could always be obtained there if you knew the right politicians." In his opinion, the very idea of the membership club during Prohibition lent an air of legitimacy to illegal activity.

> The law stayed away as long as it was quiet. There was a piano player and drums. If I remember they had a big dance hall. Now they operated after hours

but they could do it because they were a private
club. See, they would have your name on the membership roll in case of a raid. They could say that
they were having a private activity sponsored by the
membership. See, these types of membership clubs
would lend an air of legitimacy to the activity going
on but they were really operating after hours. [29]

Membership clubs were flourishing toward the end
of Prohibition. The Apex Club alone had more than
1,000 members on its roll. The sponsors bought a
house and fully renovated it; they opened it up to
create a dance floor, installed a bar near the dance
area, and offered a full lunch and dinner menu. [30] But
the growth of the clubs was curtailed by the Depression. The Apex Club closed in 1941 but reopened in
1945 just off East 55th Street, only a few doors from
the Republican Club. By then the surrounding area
had become an entertainment district. Several clubs
were located adjacent to each other, and competition
among them was fierce.

A club membership fee was usually $10. There
were no screening committee, no dues, and no club
meetings. The clubs simply provided a place to dance,
drink, and have a good time. Public dances were
forced to close at 1:00 A.M., but no permit was necessary for extended hours in private clubs. Ostensibly an
affair was for members only, but since a substantial
portion of the local public was included on the membership roll, any dance was virtually open to the public. Even so, there was a measure of control. Most
clubs had a buzzer or bell at the entrance, which allowed some discretion over admission. Buzzers became particularly popular during Prohibition (in after-

hours joints also) as a way to stall the police while illegal beverages were cleared away.[31]

A typical membership club in Cleveland, the Twelve Counts, deviated little from clubs that emerged in Buffalo, Philadelphia, Detroit, or those in Chicago described by Cayton and Drake in *Black Metropolis*.[32] Typical names included the Amicable Twelve, Loyal Twelve, Peppy Ten, Thrifty Twelve, Unique Twelve, and Pepper Ten. Most began as a clique of friends, usually ten or twelve, who decided to organize. The Twelve Counts was formed by a group of school friends who met regularly at the house of a friend who was recently separated from his wife. They organized a formal club to help defray the expenses of entertaining, and thus the club was born. To build up their treasury, the Twelve Counts initially charged admission to their parties. Patrons also paid for food and drink. After five years, the club obtained a permit and purchased a clubhouse.

Membership clubs provided activities that up to then had been the province of the jook house; one could gamble, drink, dance, and eat in either. As membership clubs grew in number, their range of offerings became more varied, increasingly catering to African-Americans' social aspirations. Nor were the clubs restricted to a particular social class. The Pyramid Club of Philadelphia, for instance, was composed of doctors, judges, attorneys, and other prominent men of the period. The elite organizations served a similar function for their members as the less prestigious clubs. The Pyramid Club's activities included lectures, banquets honoring prominent African-Americans, awards ceremonies, and art forums with prominent African-American intellectuals such as Alain Locke and Langston Hughes. As of October 12, 1940, the clubhouse offered members a fully equipped bar and grand hall. In addition to sponsoring affairs in their clubhouses, organizations rented space outside for a variety of affairs from teas to educational programs: fashion shows, recitals, organizational meetings, and dances.[33]

Membership clubs sponsored by social organizations offered a particularly wide range of affairs. They were less bound by political loyalties or public opinion than those associated with a benevolent organization or political party. They were also less constricted by the demands of political campaigning or fund raising. Nor were they obligated to share their facilities, as were the political clubs. Their primary purpose was to provide their membership with an entertaining social life.

The membership club was neither fully private nor fully public. It allowed black social life to operate, albeit with constraints from outside the community. It served too many people to be described as "private." Unlike public facilities, intervention by public officials such as police was limited, although the clubs' location and size imparted the flavor of a public arena. Like the honky-tonk, the membership club aided the transition from the jook house to the fully public institutions of today. A product of its social moment, it gradually lost its public prominence to an urban population whose demands were influenced by mass communication in an atmosphere of racist exclusion. Another institution served those demands better—the night club.

Night Clubs, Show Bars, Cabaret Parties

The origins of the American cabaret are various. Apparently similar institutions emerged in both American and European cities in the 1880s, an era marked by industrial expansion. In Europe, particularly France, the cabaret developed out of literary and artistic meeting places popular in Paris during the late 1880s. These cabarets offered a comfortable place to smoke, talk, drink, and eat. Also influenced by the French café-concert, the artistic cabaret expanded to include performances of poetry, monologue, song lyric, and short sketch.

Although there can be no doubt that cross fertilization occurred between European and American forms during and after World War I, the American cabaret has its own cultural history. Unlike the French or German cabaret the American variety was strongly influenced by both the African-American jook tradition and the minstrel theater, elements indigenous to American cultural life.

Urban whites had availed themselves of something similar to night clubs since the early 1900s. Bustanoby's, Gimbel's, and Ziegfeld's in New York all integrated elements found later in night clubs. But it was probably Florenz Ziegfeld who began the first real night club in 1915 by combining food, floor show, and dancing.[34] Exclusionary racial prejudice of the era, however, barred African-Americans totally or permitted them access only on a limited basis.

The black-owned night spots in the urban North offered entertainment, dancing, drinking, food—in brief, merriment for a price. The atmosphere was similar to that in other dance arenas, but there were differences. The jooks, rent parties, and after-hours joints discussed earlier all developed comparatively free of politics. In contrast, night clubs, membership clubs, and to some extent the early dance halls grew from alliances between politicians and "upper shadies"—individuals with substantial money and plush outward trappings, but whose wealth was gained through illegal means, usually numbers or bootlegged liquor.[35]

When Prohibition ended in 1933, state control of liquor sales set the stage for the emergence of black-owned night clubs. Unlike the jooks and after-hours places, night clubs (here also referred to as cabarets) were legal commercial establishments. They duplicated many features of the jooks, particularly the level of intimacy, but night clubs represented more formalized, sophisticated entertainment than any preceding form, and they were generally nonrestrictive in their admission policies.

The emergence of black night clubs represents the merger of two entertainment trends: the jook house, where the patrons were participants, and the popular theater, where the patrons formed an audience. In the night club a patron could enjoy a little of both. While the entertainment was in progress, all dancing stopped. The night club was the first dance arena to formally integrate elements of the theater. The same performers often appeared in both cabarets and theaters, although they varied their material for the occasion; the cabaret audience was far more tolerant than the theater audience. Though the same segregation that pervaded the white dance halls and clubs existed in white-owned night clubs, practically anyone could gain admittance to a black night club.

In Cleveland's only black-and-tan night club, the Jewish-owned Cedar Gardens, reservations signs were routinely placed on all tables from Thursday through Saturday to restrict African-Americans from the cabaret section of the club. The owner believed that blacks had little money and therefore reserved the cabaret section for whites, who were eager to spend cash to enjoy the entertainment, the food, and the Harlemlike atmosphere. The cover charge entitled a patron to a live band that took requests, dancing, and a floor show that included a chorus line, comedians, dancers, and an assortment of variety artists, including shake dancers. The chorus elements of the shows were arranged by Teddy Blackman of the famed Harlem Cotton Club and Blackbirds of 1929.

The Cedar Gardens was located on East 97th and Cedar Avenue, on the outer edges of the still-burgeoning black community. Most of the features enjoyed by whites on Thursday, Friday, and Saturday night could be enjoyed by blacks during the week. The Sunday matinee was especially popular. For a reduced fee black patrons could get the same show, music, food, and atmosphere the Gardens provided its "whites only" patrons. The reduced cover charge guaranteed a good crowd. The matinee, complete with show, could be rented for $100 and groups frequently used it as a fund-raising enterprise.[36] The policy of restricting black patrons Thursday through Saturday continued until after World War II. A former club manager explained: "They took the reserved signs down after the war because blacks had more money. They had it to spend and they were spending it."[37] As the socioeconomic profile of blacks shifted, African-American attitudes toward exclusion, segregation, and racism became more aggressive.

In larger cities like New York, Chicago, and Washington, African-Americans had access to black cabarets well before 1925.[38] There is an apparent continuity between these cabarets and entertainers' hangouts in New York during the 1880s. By the end of Prohibition a few blacks were able to become proprietors of legal establishments. Until that time the private membership club was the most sophisticated form of entertainment in most black communities. Unlike the membership club, the night club featured some form of popular artistry, either a name band, a well-known vocalist, or other entertainers such as dancers and variety artists, some of whom were club regulars.

Dancing remained important in cabaret entertainment, and it was imperative that the house band be able to take requests. The personality of the band leader also had a direct effect on business.[39] The night club served food, but if we except dancing and food, the other characteristics of the night club drew more from the popular theater than the jook tradition. In the jook continuum the participants and sponsors were often one and the same. All one had to do in a night club, however, was be there. The ownership provided setting, furnishings, entertainment, dancing, and food.

Being licensed made the night club seem legitimate, hence respectable, and therefore preferable to the jook. Its performers were better known and more sophisticated; its patrons had more money. Both performers and patrons had been influenced by urban work rhythms, jazz music, talking movies, and the post–World War I vision of a brighter future. The night club population was heterogeneous: "They were frequented by people from all walks of life including doctors, lawyers . . . businessmen . . . and musicians." The combination of money and sophistication led to stricter social standards in the night club than in earlier dance arenas. A patron perfectly acceptable in a honky-tonk, rent party, or even membership club might prove less so in the night club. The reservation signs in black clubs were used to keep out undesirables and potential troublemakers. [40]

A variety of demographic factors contributed to the black night club's beginnings. Little money, political influence, and, of course, Prohibition helped forestall their early growth. Except in larger cities, most black-owned night clubs appeared only after the end of Prohibition. [41] The price of a D5 liquor license, which permitted dancing and entertainment as well as the sale of liquor to the public, was $1,000, a real burden at the time.

The most conspicuous early black night club owners were known to have engaged in illegal activity, usually bootlegging or policy, a form of lottery that allowed bets of as little as five cents. These "upper shadies" had access to large amounts of cash, which in itself granted them real local power. They also possessed a high degree of access to the black community, thanks in particular to policy. The game was well known, and most people played with friends or relatives, which added to its air of intimacy. The numbers collector might be a neighbor trying to make ends meet. Friends would get others to play to help him out.[42]

During the Depression, policy operated on a more public scale than ever before. In Chicago and Cleveland numbers drawings became large public affairs. When most other businesses were devastated, the numbers kings still provided employment and acted as patrons of charitable causes. They became pioneers in the establishment of black businesses and, besides providing employment, influenced large numbers of African-American voters. In fact, so lucrative was the policy station that some legitimate businessmen have turned to it as their major enterprise and use their other business merely as a front.[43]

In Cleveland and Chicago the daily policy drawings were frequently held in open fields. If police pressure or bad weather prevented this, a back yard, basement, attic, or any room large enough to hold twenty-five to fifty people served as a substitute. These drawings were held three times a day or more. The property owner or tenant received about $25 for the use of his facility, a considerable sum. As many as 500 people might attend the public drawings. People would bring wares or food to sell to the crowd. Dancers often competed for coins, and everyone shared local gossip. Even those who had not played a number joined the festivities.

> The drawings used to be big public affairs, everyday in the eleventh ward, everyday people would sell bar-b-que, there was dancing, it was like a carnival or a fair, people would come to sell their wares, the police would see it but they let it happen. Sometimes there would be two or three drawings per day.[44]

Perched atop an adjacent roof, telegraph pole or tree, the lookout man would issue a call to "raise up, raise up" whenever the police threatened to stage a raid.

In the early days of policy, before 1932, the games in Cleveland were dominated by the "big four"—Rufus Jones, John B. Johnson, and Willie Richardson (African-Americans), and Frank Hodge, a white. Rufus Jones, the man believed to have brought policy from St. Louis to Cleveland, was reputed to earn a gross yearly income of $200,000, out of which he paid $36,000 in protection money and about an equal amount in salaries. This amount is considerably less than estimates for Chicago policy companies, but policy was a more recent phenomenon in Cleveland and depended on a smaller black population.[45]

As in other cities, the policy kings in Cleveland cultivated a working relationship with local ward politicians. In exchange for protection, the numbers racketeers would deliver the black vote. They would also "kick back" a percentage of their net earnings in the form of campaign contributions.[46] The combination of votes and veiled bribes made the policy kings powerful men in their localities and many viewed them as "race leaders."

The nearly certain repeal of Prohibition in 1932 threatened the profits from bootlegged liquor. The Italian mobsters who controlled the trade needed a new source of illegal income. Policy was just such an enterprise. Beginning in 1932, the Mayfield Road boys, a group of Italian-American gangsters led by "Big Angelo" Lonardo, began muscling in on policy. Similar pressures occurred in Chicago and New York, forcing the numbers kings to look elsewhere for high-profit investments. Shootings, severe beatings, and stabbings enabled the mob to extort a 40 percent protection fee from the numbers-wheel operators. While the mob did not take over the game, the "big four" were on their way out. Rufus Jones was imprisoned for income tax evasion; Willie Richardson narrowly escaped being shotgunned to death; John Johnson was shot six times and his wife killed; and Frank Hodge gave up the business voluntarily.[47] A second generation of numbers bankers took over the wheels and established the first black-owned night clubs.

The first night spot of its kind in Cleveland, the Log Cabin, opened for business in 1934. The necessary D5 license was obtained in the name of a local ward leader who had been active in Republican politics since the 1920s. The license was a political concession for "delivering the votes." His partner's name, Roger Price, was not included on the license because of his known activities in numbers. The Log Cabin was "the granddaddy of them all."[48] It was

> a place of remarkable beauty with its artistic wall hangings, rich rugs, polished bar, and dainty waitresses . . . the new night spot was frequented by people from all walks of life . . . The Log Cabin billed itself as a "little bit of Harlem" featured such entertainers from New York's Negro metropolis as Mary C. "Diamond Tooth" Perry and quickly became the center of Cleveland's black and tan sporting crowd.[49]

This pattern was repeated all over. Numbers man Benny Mason opened the Blue Grass Club in Cleveland in 1935. In 1938, the R&C Chatterbox Club was opened by prominent numbers men John H. Ballard

and Horace Pearson, brother of the Log Cabin owner;
wheel operators John B. Johnson and Willie Richardson opened the Douglass Club. Jack Oliver commented: "All the Negroes that I knew who owned
joints where people could go, all those Negroes were
numbers bookers. All the big Negro numbers men had
places. In fact there was only one club owner who didn't
get his money to open a joint through numbers."[50]

In Cleveland, more than a dozen well-known clubs
featured entertainment, dancing, and nightly shows.
True night clubs, they boasted well-attired interiors
with tables and dance floors, and often more than one
bar. Similar clubs proliferated in other cities with substantial black populations.[51]

The numbers kings figured moderately in the flow
of cash in Cleveland and more prominently in larger
cities. Night clubs, in fact, were only one type of black-
owned business financed by the rackets; restaurants,
insurance companies, and grocery stores were equally
indebted to policy money. As one interviewee put it:

> If you think times are hard for black people now
> you should have seen it back then. Black people
> didn't have anything and if anybody wanted to start
> a business or a club or a dance hall they had to bor-
> row money. Who do you supposed they had to bor-
> row it from—the racketeers and the numbers
> kings. The banks didn't loan black people money
> back then.[52]

The night club enjoyed a long reign in large cities,
but in Cleveland and other small cities its foundation
began to crumble in less than three decades. Unionization, entertainment taxes, and urban decay all contributed to the cabaret's demise. The American Guild

of Variety Artists (AGVA) limited the variety artists who could perform in night clubs and raised their rates. Cleveland performers who later became AGVA members told me that Cleveland and other cities had enjoyed good local entertainment. Audience members could be called on the floor to perform, and frequently were. Talent was plentiful, salaries low, and entertainment was cheap. Although AGVA had been formed in the 1930s, the unionization effort among African-American entertainers got underway in Cleveland only around 1940. At the time union dues were $75 per year per person, out of the range of most local black talent, but for a reduced rate they could join as a group.[53]

The reaction to AGVA unionization efforts from local performers was mixed; the union curtailed all freelancing, which put some entertainers out of work. Before the union many worked for $5 per night or tips, or whatever the club management would agree to. After unionization, entertainers earned $12 per night, but they couldn't work in some places and many black-owned clubs were nonunion.[54] The union placed other restrictions on black entertainers, particularly on out-of-town engagements. Nonunion entertainers were forced to secure a permit from the local AGVA agent in charge of the district, and permit fees ranged from $50 to $75 for a week-long engagement—often two to three times the entertainer's weekly salary.

The 20 percent entertainment or cabaret tax dealt another blow to the clubs. Club owners responded by increasing liquor and admission prices. Former club owners complained bitterly about the tax. "The tax drove us out," one former club owner told me.[55] Some places closed immediately. Though the tax was repealed after World War II, many clubs did not survive that long.

After the war, increased income enabled some black workers to move away from inner-city communities; the old areas deteriorated, burdened by rising unemployment and crime. The black patrons who had moved away grew reluctant to journey back for entertainment, and white patronage also dwindled. One former club owner expressed his plight this way: "You know whites have always loved black entertainment and they still do. They just can't go into the black community any more because of crime."[56] Television also helped finish the clubs. This new medium began taking a share of the weekend audience of the early 1950s; it provided less expensive entertainment and was seldom the focus of moral and religious objections. In fact, television was praised as being home and family centered, compared with night clubs.

Existing clubs gradually closed their doors and few new ones opened, but the appetite for cabaret entertainment remained unsatisfied. Desire soon found an outlet. If revelers could not find cabarets, they would make one of their own. The cabaret party featured all the offerings of the cabaret on a one-night-only basis. It could be given by a club, a neighborhood group, or by an individual. Unlike the jook forms, cabaret parties were not given in a private residence; the sponsors usually rented a public dance hall. Tickets were printed and sold at least four weeks in advance, although guests could buy them at the door. If a group organized the affair, each member would sell a minimum number of tickets. The sponsors advertised with poster placards tacked on telephone poles and buildings or placed in local merchants' display windows, and with announcements on the local black radio station. All that remained was food and entertainment. Cooking was generally the task of volunteers, but cooks were hired if volunteers were unavailable. Entertainment could be secured from local talent, irrespective of union status, thus avoiding union problems. The final necessary feature of the cabaret, liquor, was provided in a fashion that circumvented liquor licensing. "BYOB" in small type on each ticket and advertising placard informed the participants that it was necessary to "bring your own bottle." The cabaret party sold "setups," a plastic cup with ice and a soft drink, usually soda, ginger ale, or cola. The price of a ticket bought admission, a table, entertainment by a variety artist, and dancing to a live band. Depending on the arrangements, admission could include food, drink, or "setup," though food was usually sold separately.

The success of the cabaret party depended on the sociability of the group. More than the night club, the cabaret party was an interdependent network of friends and associates. In small, though significant, measure the cabaret party returned to the patrons the independent sense of cultural participation that had been traditional in the jook. Things had come full circle; once again the sponsors and the patrons were one and the same.

Sometime between 1955 and the early 1960s, cabaret night clubs disappeared entirely. No other dance arena provided black communities with a similar level of community expression. They could not be replaced by other commercial entertainment centers like bars or the discotheques that were developing during the early 1960s, or the discos of the 1970s and 1980s.

Dancin' in the Streets

A block party was an affair in which a city block, usually a side street, was closed to traffic in order to permit dancing. It can be defined as an informal street festival that provided a public arena for spontaneous participation free of charge. It both reflected and reinforced a sense of community, particularly among the African-American working classes.

In Baltimore, Chicago, and Philadelphia, block parties were often tied to "block beautification" or cleanup campaigns. Commonly sponsored by newspapers such as the *Chicago Defender,* these block parties encouraged middle-class values of achievement and pride. Dancing was seldom their primary focus. But another type of block party developed in Cleveland. The dances began in the summer of 1945 and were held throughout the black eleventh ward. They were sponsored by Jean Murrell Capers, city councilmember for the ward, as part of her campaign.[57] The block parties allowed the candidate-sponsor to meet voters outside the formal setting typical of political campaigns. This familiarity enhanced the effectiveness of other campaign efforts, such as posters or paid political announcements. Moreover, block parties reached the youth, the future voters, providing the sponsor with a solid base of support for years to come.

Since it was illegal to use public property for political purposes, the city recreational department possesses no applications for block dance permits in the name of Jean Capers. Ostensibly, the dances were given for recreational purposes by neighborhood individuals or associations. The local street club would obtain the permit after Mrs. Capers, or her campaign manager, asked the club for an endorsement. If the neighborhood had no street club, it could form one for the occasion. If that approach didn't work, a resident was recruited to obtain the permit.[58]

Unlike any postemancipation dance arena except debutante balls, the block party could involve the entire family. It provided the first experience with public dancing for many young people in the eleventh ward, and helped imprint on them a strong sense of their identity as community members. In fact, the block party was the most homogeneous of all forms of public dancing. Most participants lived on the block and, like most neighbors, tended to share the same economic status. Occasionally residents from neighboring streets attended. In Cleveland the block dances were held on alternating streets within the political ward until the entire ward was covered, thus ensuring that ward residents knew of at least one block party given by the councilperson.[59]

There was no admission charge for a block party. Because it was held outside, observers could view the activities from a porch or window. Refreshments were available from either a neighborhood store or a local home. Participants could simply carry refreshments from their house or apartment and relax on their porch, on a parked car, or on a folding chair. All age groups participated, but some activities were age-specific. Younger people tended to do most of the dancing. Indeed, the main activity at the block dance was dancing, unlike other entertainment forms that sponsored drinking, gambling, or professional performers. The dances nevertheless generated considerable activity among the nondancing adults. There was much good-natured talk. Card games such as "bid whist," checkers, and dominoes were played on porches or just outside the dance area.

A phonograph supplied the music for the block dance. Sound equipment in the back of a station wagon was connected to a gramophone-shaped speaker mounted on the roof. It played the latest 45 or 78 rpm records that were popular in the black community. At regular intervals, the music paused for campaign announcements or a personal dedication.

A community resident, always a male who owned the necessary equipment, was hired as a disc jockey. The fee for his services was around $15 per hour, which included the equipment, the operator, and his records. Participants also contributed records. They were instructed to print their names or initials on the record label for identification, and at the end of the affair the discs were returned to their owners. Electricity for the sound equipment was provided by a resident who lived near the center of the block. The councilperson carried an extension cord purchased specifically for hooking up the music. If no one volunteered his electricity, payment was offered, usually $2 or $3. Frequently, volunteers were happy to make this contribution to the community event.

Older adults, those with children old enough to participate, rarely danced. Instead, they flanked the perimeter and encouraged the younger dancers, particularly when someone demonstrated a posture or gesture esteemed in African-American culture. Onlookers shouted encouragement: "Work with it, baby," "burn it," or "cut his mouth out." Those who actually danced formed an inner circle. The bulk of the crowd surrounded them in an oval that lined the street; the crowd often spilled over onto the pavement. The dancers would make their way through the crowd to the open space at the center.

Block parties usually took place on the weekend, though during the summer months they might occur during the week. Setting up the affair usually began around 6:00 P.M., well before dark. All through traffic was blocked off. The loudspeaker announced the opening of the event. Once a sufficient crowd gathered, a few announcements were made, and then the affair was underway. Unlike other forms of public dancing, block parties were rarely announced ahead of time, and this contributed to the air of spontaneity. The dance continued no more than half an hour after sunset, and still most parties managed to last almost three hours.

The block dances frequently culminated in a contest of dancing ability. At the end of the season, the winners from each block would meet for a final challenge in a public or rented hall. During the course of the eliminations, handbills printed with campaign announcements for the local councilperson circulated among the crowd; between eliminations there were announcements. These contests were crowded with eager parents, friends, and relatives—mostly female. In competitive categories based on age, contestants were judged by audience applause. The presentation of contestants on an elevated stage enhanced the theatrical aspect of the affair.

The appearance of block dances in Cleveland coincides with the post–World War II migration of African-Americans from the South. The new arrivals brought their culture with them. Spontaneous competitive dancing has long been a feature of African-American dance culture. It was customary for at least one unscheduled dancing contest to "break out" during the course of a block party. This competition might settle a dispute with a rival, or merely demonstrate superb dancing ability. In any case, the competitors would try to outmaneuver each other with impressive embellishments. These competitions were the high point of the evening. Generally, when a contest began, observers would leave the sidelines to get a better view and possibly learn a few new steps themselves. Thus the dance movement perpetuated itself in the community.

Several dances at the block party were new versions of older dances. These included poppin' the hips (a version of the old plantation dance known as snake hips), the bop (a new version of the lindy hop), and the mashed potatoes (a dance requiring movements similar to those in the Charleston). Other dances included the horse, which consisted of rapidly crossing foot movements, and the slop, which appeared in two versions; the older version was more flat-footed and involved more hip movement. Two group line dances were popular, the madison and the birdland.[60] In both dances, men and women lined up facing each other and performed the same steps while a couple or individuals danced between the lines, exhibiting their proficiency and creativity. A favorite movement for dancing down the center was the camel walk, a step similar to the Ghanian Adowa, originally a funeral dance performed by the Ashanti people.

Unlike the other dance forms, the block party had no "regulars," so gaining status at the dance depended on what happened at the moment. What happened, particularly for the youth, was based almost entirely on dancing ability. Individuals who received dedications of tunes during the evening gained prestige, as did anyone whose name was mentioned over the loudspeaker. The disc jockeys, and even those who personally knew the disc jockeys (or appeared to), were also allotted some status.

Fine clothing was of negligible importance. Since the dance took place on the pavement, the participants were bound to become dirty. The only available seating other than folding chairs was provided by parked cars, front stairs, or curbs, which were also dirty. Acrobatic dancing styles frequently required dancers to touch the ground with more than their feet, as in a split, so there was little point in wearing good clothes. People often dropped what they were doing when they heard a block party starting up and changed into "dancin' clothes"—soft-soled, well-worn shoes or sneakers and old, loose-fitting pants or skirts. The restrictive skirt fashions of the period were readily discarded. Of course, some people attended block parties well dressed, and they drew attention. But status in the block party required more than clothing.

At the block dance one could publicly exhibit dance movements approved by the African-American working class. It was like dancing in one's own home or in the home of friends. The block party provided youth

with an intermediary arena in which to test their proficiency before moving on to more public dance events.
The participants particularly enjoyed having the entire
street blocked off. They enjoyed taking over the pavement from automobiles. Street dancing was especially
popular among the younger participants. Playing in
the street was forbidden by parents, school, and state,
but the block party temporarily permitted the forbidden, which made it all the more fun. Claiming the
street was a territorial triumph.

The block dances temporarily expanded the living
space of the neighborhood. Once the function was underway, previously hidden community relations began
to surface. Courtship and community rivalries became
visible. Rivalries among the youth were often handled
through dancing. An invitation by a rival to dance was
a challenge. Sometimes the challenge was nonverbal;
the challenger merely broke in on the rival and partner, pushing the partner away and confronting the rival directly. In the course of dancing, the object was to
display the most advanced repertoire of movement
possible. As each rival demonstrated his or her best
steps, the winner was determined by the response of
the immediate audience. The vanquished competitor
slunk away, effectively silenced and shamed. The winner was congratulated and vigorously praised, and the
observers learned some new dance steps. In the community terminology, if one had effectively handled a
rival, put him or her to shame on the dance floor, one
had "cut his (or her) mouth out." It was a great source
of self-esteem and a salient feature of each block party.

Because it brought community relationships into
the open, the block dance could serve as a vent for

community hostilities, especially among the young. The political sponsorship was aware of that possibility and devised a means to diminish its likelihood. Between 1945 and 1959 street gangs were a problem in most major cities. Cleveland was no exception. Their proliferation made the location of block dances a matter of strategy. The dances were staggered according to neighborhood to allow a cooling-off period for hot tempers left over from the last dance. For example, if the last block dance was held in the northwest section of the ward, the next would be held in the southeast.

Street gang activity contributed to another feature of the block party—its spontaneity. Because block dances were never announced ahead of time, rival groups were unable to prepare a major invasion into enemy territory. Confining the party primarily to street residents minimized unpleasantness or fighting. Even so, gang members sometimes attended block parties in order to touch off a confrontation. If someone asked the wrong girl to dance, or "cut someone's mouth out," a fight was certain. Gang members took pride in their dancing ability. In his study of the Vice Lords, a Chicago street gang, R. Lincoln Keiser observes:

> Vice Lords value soul. To tell someone he has soul is a compliment, while to say he has a "hole in his soul" is a definite criticism. There are certain social situations in which judgments are made in terms of soul. These are contexts involving music. Dancing is even more important in Vice Lord life. Almost all Vice Lords take intense pride in their dancing ability, and lose few opportunities to demonstrate it. [61]

A gang member who couldn't dance well would feel incomplete; the status of the entire group might suffer.

After only one summer of block dances the residents of the eleventh ward came to accept them as a regular feature of community life. At first there was some minor grumbling, chiefly from people unable to park their cars or drive on the street during the dance. But the overall enjoyment of everyone won out over the minor inconvenience, and residents with cars eventually made the small sacrifice in good humor.

Black Elite Affairs

In contrast to working-class dance arenas, African-American elite forms—debutante balls and dinner dances—have been sponsored primarily by voluntary associations and reflect a much different set of values and tastes. They are not simply more sophisticated versions of forms that emerged among the black working classes; they are largely derived from Euro-American tradition and reflect a degree of identification with, or aspiration to, the dominant culture.

Even in times of economic difficulty the black elite have more money to spend on social activities than do their less fortunate brethren. They have always provided elaborate settings in which to dance and make merriment. Yet the culture-creating efforts of the black elite have not been remarkably innovative; nor have they further developed the working-class strain of African-American culture. According to sociologist E. Franklin Frazier, a dynamic cultural tension between the classes is rooted in the black elite's rejection of core black culture and this elite's rejection by whites.

These tensions drive the black elite toward cultural structures that enable them to accrue status and exhibit authority.[62]

In the years preceding emancipation, "elite slaves" gave affairs and balls modeled on those of their well-to-do masters. These balls were generally held by urban slaves, often with the assistance of their masters, and rivaled white affairs in the degree of elaborate preparation. It is debatable how much influence African high culture could have exerted in the Americas. Certainly there were slaves familiar with the courts of African kings, a tradition in which the court and its attendants would have the best of everything; they would know high-culture fashion, makeup, music, art, and dance. They could have composed a significant portion of the slaves who were personal servants to influential whites, but their effect on black culture in the New World, if any, remains a matter of speculation. The elite slaves in Montgomery, Alabama, gave a yearly Christmas ball at which formal attire was required. This affair was sponsored by a slave club that enlisted the mayor of Montgomery to petition the city council for permission to hold the affair, and to keep the city lamps burning late to provide the departing participants with light. Embossed invitations were sent to the elite slaves and the better class of whites.[63]

During the years following emancipation, elite affairs served several purposes. One was debunking racist notions about Negroes; blacks believed themselves to be "uplifting the race" by adopting upper-class behavior. They hoped to elicit approval from the general public and to demonstrate that blacks were worthy participants in the American dream. Second, the vol-

untary associations that sponsored these affairs provided elite African-Americans with alternatives to a
white society that denied them access.[64] Third, these
functions raised funds. During the post–Civil War
period the black elite was more race conscious and
progressive than it would ever be again. Its positive
response to the needs of the freedmen was intensified
by post-Reconstruction black codes that lumped all
people of African descent into the same legal category.
These early fund-raising efforts were numerous and
well chronicled.

The characteristics of the black elite or "Negro
bourgeoisie" have changed almost as frequently as the
conditions that govern the lives of African-Americans.
Therefore it is necessary to redefine this group as we
examine its dance institutions. The black bourgeoisie
is not a bourgeoisie at all in the traditional Marxist sense. Rather, it is an elite in the context of the
African-American experience. At times high status
was rooted primarily in color delineations. In other instances, income, property ownership, occupation, education, wealth, and contact with whites have played a
part in determining the elite.

In cities like Chicago before World War I and Cleveland before World War II, a limited number of black
individuals formed an elite as defined by white standards; they were primarily professionals with white
clientele, merchants, entrepreneurs, skilled crafts-
men, even headwaiters in exclusive establishments.[65]
A remarkable number of them were light in color. The
migration northward changed all that, both expanding
and redefining the elite. This new group did not depend on white clientele for its status, but began ac-

quiring wealth by serving the growing community of black migrants and working-class individuals; wealth became the basis of their status. This new elite was less educated than the old but its income roughly equal.

Lifestyle also distinguished the older elite from the new. The older community had only limited contact with the black masses, and many were native to the city in which they lived. The new elite emerged out of the migration. Sheer numbers enabled this new elite to sponsor large social events such as formal dances and balls. There had been exclusive social groups among the old elite, which in Cleveland dated back as far as 1869, but the community was too small to support major activity on a regular basis.[66]

The number of black elite organizations in Cleveland began increasing around 1900. A well-known club was the Caterers Association, a men's club formed on the basis of occupational association. Its development over time was typical. Most of the founding members were prominent waiters and caterers, representatives of the old elite. They dominated the club initially, but as the social climate ripened they were gradually replaced.[67] The replacements— businessmen, lawyers, and other professionals as well as "upper shadies"—depended on the black community for financial support as well as social contacts.

The occupational structure of most northern black communities was less diverse before the migration than afterward, and social life reflected the change. A network of voluntary social groupings began to establish itself, closely tied to the new prosperity that resulted from the increasing industrial output of the period. The elite formed associations designed to demonstrate their cultural superiority. The Royal Vagabonds, for example, the oldest organization of its kind in Cleveland, was founded by a group of recent college graduates. They sought to create a cooperative network with access to professional contacts and those of similar class. These younger men were not admitted to the more prestigious (and older) Metropolitan Club. There were thirty or so original Royal Vagabonds, from neighboring towns such as Akron. The core of this group had met at Howard University. All had finished school, chiefly in law, medicine, or dentistry, and they used their college contacts as a source to recruit new members.

A college degree, out of reach for most African-Americans, was and remains a significant criterion for admission. Equally important are professional status and income. Most contemporary elite organizations have a membership drawn from the professions of law, medicine, dentistry, education, social work, and the like. Admission criteria were established in the early days of these associations, and changed very little in the years that followed; however, the early associations had fewer college graduates than those that developed after World War I. Most have formal procedures for obtaining new members. Current members nominate friends or acquaintances they think are qualified. The membership then determines whether the nominee's family life is stable and his or her principles compatible with those of the club.[68] Being in good moral standing is important. Few elite organizations, for instance, have members whose parents are unmarried.

Before World War I, elite organizations engaged in numerous fund-raising efforts to aid less fortunate blacks. More recently these efforts have trailed off. In many cases their original goals and ideals of racial uplift have degenerated into hollow posturing.[69] Instead of providing means whereby African-Americans could seek cultural and social alternatives, they provide the elite with vehicles to demonstrate their own prestige and authority. They shield themselves behind a conservative Eurocentric model of culture and generally disdain African-based culture. The black bourgeoisie sees its affairs as an expression of upward mobility, differentiating them from the masses of African-Americans.

As the twentieth century progressed, the weaknesses of "racial uplift" as perceived by the black elite have become more apparent. The rise of black consciousness in the 1960s left the black elite largely defensive. Many organizations dropped cotillions from their program and substituted dinner dances, but that substitution drew them no closer to the working-class community. The restricted admission, the cost of the affairs, and the location of the site, all discouraged working-class blacks as participants. The price of the debutante ball is beyond the budget of most working-class blacks. In January 1980, the fee to present a child was $500. Only members of the sponsoring organization and their friends could obtain tickets. Each "presenting family" is charged the cost of two tickets, and must pay the club $500. Moreover, each presenting family is expected to provide a hotel suite so that guests and friends may relax in a private atmosphere. Special clothing (evening gowns and tuxedoes) and other accoutrements of these grand affairs add to the total cost.

The site of the affair is carefully chosen to reflect the esthetic values of the organization. Usually the newest or a highly prestigious older hall or hotel is selected. Sometimes a hotel is selected on the basis of a special feature, such as a spiral staircase or an indoor pool. Esthetic considerations aside, the site functions to restrict working-class accessibility. Many blacks limit weekend activity to their own community.[70] An expensive journey into unfamiliar surroundings in order to be socially embarrassed is hardly worth the trouble.

The staging of these affairs has varied little across time or region. The first black cotillion in Cleveland was modeled on a cotillion traditional to Birmingham, Alabama. At these affairs the young individual demonstrates his or her readiness to assume membership within the elite. In this respect the cotillion can be viewed as a rite of passage. The ideals of manners, gentility, and concern for social graces are acted out through dance, costume, and staging. Each facet of the production exhibits approved attitudes toward achievement, family, male-female roles, property relations, and class.[71]

The Cleveland cotillion begins with guests arriving at the appointed hour. They are welcomed by a receiving line in the lobby or a central location. The proceedings are then formally called to order by a master or mistress of ceremonies, someone of high status and good reputation. Though an "upper shady" may have attained the necessary wealth, he lacks the respectability. In past years the assistant superintendent for curriculum and instruction of the Cleveland Board of Education and the general referee of the Cleveland Municipal Court have filled this post. Interestingly, gender is less important in filling this position than professional achievement, moral uprightness, and acceptance by the professional community at large.

The guests are then formally welcomed by the president of the sponsoring organization, followed by a formal recognition of special guests or the presenting parents. These presentations and acknowledgments allow time for the participants in the procession to line up for the grand entrance. The procession is a symbolic embodiment of both the life cycle and values of the group. All ages participate. Very young children, from age five to eleven—known as "pages," "flower girls," "rosebuds," or some other diminutive designation—lead the procession. The number of children determines whether an older group, usually age twelve to fifteen, will follow. These are "junior debs," "squires," or a similar label that indicates their intermediate status. Usually the escorts follow next; the debs remain out of sight until their presentation. Once the procession is complete and participants are in their places forming a large semicircle, the presentation of the debutantes begins.

The presentation involves two steps: first, a prestigious individual other than the master of ceremonies calls each girl's name individually; the deb then moves to the center of the semicircle, curtsies, is met by her father or a male surrogate, and presented by him to her escort, who takes her hand and leads her to a designated place on the floor. When all the debutantes have been presented to the audience and to their es-

corts, the debutantes dance with their fathers and
then with their escorts. All members of the cotillion
then waltz. When the opening dance is over, they return to their places in the semicircle. The presentation of the charity donation or scholarship follows the
waltz. The donation is a conspicuous symbol of the
black elite's concern for "those who have less," and is
designed to offset the highly restrictive nature of the
cotillion.

Dancing at these affairs is observably different from
that found in working-class arenas. There may be
some unrestrained dancing, but it is not emphasized.
Sociologist Nathan Hare described the dancing of the
black elite:

> At exclusive gatherings of top society folk, you can
> now sit back and watch some 20 couples lined up
> on a patio, busily executing the Wobble and the
> Watusi. They are unaware that a good many such
> dance crazes were imported from Southern back-
> woods, as well as Miami and Baltimore. Local "pro-
> fessionals" acquire community fame for their
> unique version of the "twist," which they perfect to
> demonstrate how much they are in the "modern
> swing of things." But since they are generally
> latecomers to the twist, having learned it first from
> whites, their styles are a burlesque of the pioneer
> Negro twisters.[72]

Debutante balls usually solicit donations from
local businesses or individuals, although in recent
years larger businesses have declined to contribute.[73]
In exchange patrons receive an endorsement in the
program booklet, which usually takes the form of con-
gratulations to the debutante from the patron. It has

been difficult to solicit support from white businesses, and these affairs are usually totally black supported. Often black businesses that serve as sponsors have a relative, either a debutante or junior deb, involved in the program.

The formal affairs of the elite encourage and objectify class division in the black community. On the other hand, they have become odd anachronisms cut off from broader black culture. In much the same way that cotillions function as rites of passage for elite youth, dance parties function for the working-class adolescent. [74] Both affairs provide prearranged social contact with peers and the opportunity to emulate adult behavior. They mark the movement of the young away from home-centered activity. For elite youth the cotillion symbolizes an additional aspect of adult life— lofty division from core culture.

POSTSCRIPT

LIKE ALL social institutions, black dance arenas reflect the history, sociocultural tenor, and power relations of their era. Yet by no means were they passive reflectors; each left its stamp on the culture at large. No institution, however, equaled the importance of the classic jook and its derivative forms. For it is in the jook that core black culture—its food, language, community fellowship, mate selection, music, and dance—found sanctuary. It was the jook that furnished African-American dance culture with a bridge over troubled water. The jook, like the blues and the church, provided a model that shaped what came after it. Further, the jook has provided theater artists with a rich fund of material: "The Negro theater built up by the Negro is based on Jook situations, with women, gambling, fighting, and drinking."[1]

Working-class dance arenas provided African-Americans with a bulwark against white cultural domination. They also created an atmosphere in which change and innovation flourished. But that may not always be the case. Today jooks and honky-tonks are practically nonexistent, membership clubs are few and far between, rent parties rarely occur, dance halls have become discos accommodating the young and marginal, and the cabaret night club is no longer with us. What is left? After-hours joints and cabaret parties, clubs and bars. Private house parties, discos, show

173

bars, and nonentertainment bars dominate the contemporary urban scene.[2] As sophisticated and glittering as these may appear, black core culture is deteriorating.

Its loyalties divided, the black elite has given little support to any African-based dance institutions. "The black bourgeoisie, they don't go in them joints or to rent parties."[3] And although the African-American heritage continues to be a creative source for white popular culture, the strength of that heritage is waning among city-dwelling blacks. Increasingly, African-Americans have entered the dance halls and public dancing arenas of urban whites.

Following the 1960s and the closing of the last cabarets, again facing a need for cultural redefinition, African-Americans once more looked toward Africa. That too was short-lived, as the forces of post-1960s conservatism blew away the spirit of that period, leaving Euro-American cultural domination less challenged. Disco, the glittering dance arena of the 1970s, was highly commercial and youth-oriented. Not all blacks were seduced by its lure, but some were. Many continued to attend the after-hours places, but their children, particularly the upwardly mobile, were less inclined to do so.

For blacks who see dance as more than mere entertainment, disco proved distasteful. Aside from encouraging the most insensitive uses of African-American dance movement, the acrobatics reflect a decadent, alienated culture. One contemporary scholar described disco's effect on black dance this way:

Consider the disco sound which has been so successfully merchandized. Alienated, depersonalized dancers invade the floor, supposedly free of their inhibitions, but quietly imbibing the grotesqueness of their motions, distorted by the illusion of light, sound, and motion. Technology has eliminated the creative spontaneity of dance and the celebrative, ritualistic expression we enjoy as we watch excellent dancers.

If this quote is reminiscent of one by Eldridge Cleaver, it is because both men observed different manifestations of the same phenomenon. Cleaver described contemporary disco in its cradle; Lynch comments on the recent variety.[4]

The cabaret party, on the other hand, maintained the urban core culture in all its richness. With easy community access, a format adaptable to individual or group sponsorship, it was a dance arena that kept culture in the hands of the participants. Subsequent dance arenas have yet to match the cabaret party's sophistication.

Although no attempt has been made here to thoroughly document the African origins of African-American dance, much of what we have examined bears striking resemblance to cultural institutions among blacks in other parts of the world. What of the "native bars" that have developed all over Africa? They offer dancing, recorded music, and soft as well as alcoholic beverages. "Native beer," as it is called in Kenya, is homemade from the fruit of the baoba tree and drunk in "native bars."[5] The patrons appear to be people in transition from village to urban life. Similar institutions exist through African and the Caribbean.

Finally, what of the South African "shebeen," which bears a remarkable resemblance to the African-

American after-hours joint? In both institutions patrons are served in the owner's home, the liquor trade
is conducted surreptitiously, ownership is not gender-
specific, and dancing and music are a large part of the
attraction. If there is such a thing as a South African
jook continuum, the shebeen is part of it. Estimates
put their number at 4,000 in Soweto alone, where
there is only one legal bar.[6] Soweto blacks cannot obtain licenses to open clubs, just as American blacks
could not only a few generations ago.

The parallels may be the product of similar conditions. The shebeen serves the South African towns-
men in much the same fashion as the jook forms
served African-Americans. Both groups have suffered
under white supremacy. Examined in light of the colonial model, other similarities emerge that lend themselves to a pan-African interpretation of cultural development.[7] That, however, is the subject of another
study.

There are still some who ignore the history of the
black working class; others are inclined to label black
culture and social life "pathological." As far from truth
as that may now appear, it has not always been obvi-
ous. In spite of enslavement, disfranchisement, up-
rooting, and unemployment, African-Americans have
carved out a rich cultural heritage for themselves that
has sustained and replenished white America as well.
How long that will continue is a question that those
concerned with the preservation of black culture can
only ponder.

NOTES

CHAPTER ONE

1. John S. Mbiti, *African Religion and Philosophy* (New York: Doubleday, 1970). Robert Farris Thompson, *African Art in Motion* (Los Angeles: University of California Press, 1974); Peggy Harper, "Dance in Nigeria," *Ethnomusicology* 13, 280–95; Odette Blum, "Dance in Ghana," *Dance Perspectives* 56 (Winter 1973).

2. Michel Huet, *The Dance, Art and Ritual of Africa* (New York: Pantheon Books, 1978).

3. Measurement of slave ship *Brookes* from Thomas Clarkson, *An abstract of the Evidence delivered before a Selected Committee of the House of Commons in the years 1790 and 1791 on the Part of the Petitioners for the Abolition of the Slave Trade* (London: James Phillips, George Yard, Lombard Street, 1791), 37. Captain Theophilus Conneau, *A Slavers Log Book* (New York: Avon Books, 1976), ix, 312–15. See Daniel P. Mannix and Malcolm Cowley, *Black Cargoes* (New York: Viking Press, 1962), 105.

4. Thomas Clarkson, *History of the Rise, Progress and Accomplishment of the African Slave Trade by the British Parliament* (London: John W. Parker, West Strand, 1839), 304–5.

5. Clarkson, *History*, 304–5. "These meals says Mr. Falconbrige consists of rice, yams and horse-beans, with now and then a little beef and bread. After meals they are made to jump in their irons. This is called 'dancing' by the slave dealers. In every ship he has been desired 'to flog such as would not jump.' He had generally a cat of nine tails in his hand among the women and the chief mate, he believes,

another among the men." Mr. Ecroide Claxton sailed for Africa in 1788 as a surgeon aboard the slave vessel *Young Hero* (34).

6. George Howe, "The Last Slave-Ship," *Scribners Magazine*, July 1890, 123, 124, 114.

7. Edmund B. D'Auvergne, *Human Livestock* (London: Grayson and Grayson, 1933), 69–70.

8. George Frances Dow, *Slave Ships and Slaving* (Westport, Conn.: Negro Universities Press), 50.

9. "The Sorrow of Yamba; Or, the Negro Woman's Lamentation" (1790), Cornell University Rare Book Collection, (Cheap Repository), Ithaca, N.Y.

10. Dow, *Slave Ships and Slaving*, 50, 84–85.

11. Ibid., 241.

12. Mannix and Cowley, *Black Cargoes*, 125–26. A passenger sailing on board the illegal slaver *Boa Morte* as its supernumerary doctor in 1849 writes: "We had half of the gangs on decks for exercise and they danced and sang under the drivers whips, but were far from spritely" (Dow, *Slave Ships and Slaving*, 238).

13. John Miller Chernoff, *African Rhythm and African Sensibility* (Chicago: University of Chicago Press, 1979), 50.

14. Mannix and Cowley, *Black Cargoes*, 117.

15. William E. B. DuBois, *The Suppression of the African Slave Trade to the United States of America, 1638–1879* (reprint, New York: Dover Publications, 1970), 109–18; see also Philip D. Curtin, *The Atlantic Slave Trade: A Census*, (Madison: University of Wisconsin Press, 1969), 72–74; and Mannix and Cowley, *Black Cargoes*, 191–262. Dena J. Epstein, *Sinful Tunes and Spirituals*, (Urbana: University of Illinois Press), 188.

16. LeRoi Jones, *Blues People: Negro Music in White America* (New York: Morrow, 1963), 18. See also Eileen Southern, *The Music of Black Americans: A History* (New York: W. W. Norton, 1971), 179; Janheinz Jahn, *Muntu*

(New York: Grove Press, 1961), 223; and Miles Fischer, *Negro Slave Songs in the United States* (Secaucus, N.J.: Citadel Press, 1978), 21, 120, 156.

17. Fernando Ortiz, *Los Instrumentos de la Musica Afrocubana*, vol. 3 (Havana: Publicaciones de la Direccion de Cultura Del Ministerio De Educacion, 1952), 367–78.

18. Ibid., 376.

19. Frederick Law Olmsted, *A Journey in the Seaboard Slave States* (New York, 1856), 449.

20. Rupert Sargent Holland, ed., *Letters and Diary of Laura M. Towne. Written from the Sea Islands of South Carolina, 1862–1884.* (Cambridge: Riverside Press, 1912), 20.

21. Sterling Stuckey, *Slave Culture: Nationalist Theory and the Foundations of Black America* (New York: Oxford University Press, 1987), 3–83. Stuckey discusses possibilities for the "ring shout," a widespread plantation dance, as the primary mechanism through which interethnic assimilation occurred. For another account of the ring shout, see Lydia Parrish, *Slave Songs of the Georgia Sea Islands* (New York: Creative Age Press, 1942).

22. "Management of Negroes," *DeBow's Review* 11 (July–December 1851): 372.

23. Edward R. Turner, *The Negro in Virginia* (New York: Hastings House Publishers, 1940), 90.

24. Robert Farris Thompson, "An Aesthetic of the Cool: West African Dance," *African Forum* 2, no. 2 (Fall 1966): 13.

25. Alice Bauer and Raymond Bauer, "Day to Day Resistance to Slavery," *Journal of Negro History* 10 (October 1942): 389. Epstein, *Sinful Tunes and Spirituals,* 41.

26. Foby, "Management of Servants," *Southern Cultivator* 11 (August 1853): 227–28.

27. George Rawick, *South Carolina Narratives, American Slavery* part 3 of (Westport, Conn.: Greenwood Press, 1972), 34. Georgia Writers project, WPA, *Drums and Shad-*

ows (Athens: University of Georgia Press, 1940), 179–80.

28. Abe C. Ravity, "John Pierpont and the Slaves' Christmas," *Phylon* 21 (Winter 1960): 384. For another description of slave activity during Christmas, see Jacob Stroyer, *My Life in the South* (Salem: Salem Observer Book and Job Print, 1885), 47–48.

29. Rawick *South Carolina Narratives,* 56, 38.

30. Eugene Genovese, *Roll Jordan Roll: The World the Slaves Made* (New York: Random House, 1976), 574. See also Jean Caldwell, "Christmas in Old Natchez," *Journal of Mississippi History* 21 (October 1959): 362.

31. "Management of Negroes," *DeBow's Review* 19 (July–December 1855): 362.

32. Louise-Clark Pyrnelle, *Diddie Dumps and Tot or Plantation Child Life* (New York: Harper and Brothers, 1882), 34–35. For a description of a Christmas holiday, see Caldwell, "Christmas in Natchez," 257–70; see also James Battle Auirette, *The Old Plantation: How We Lived in the Great House and Calvin before the War* (New York: F. Tennyson Neely, 1901), 193.

33. "Diary of John Carmichael Jenkins," December 27, 1845, in Louisiana State University Department of Archives. For other examples of the promise of Christmas used to discipline slaves, see Pyrnelle, *Diddie Dumps,* 30–43.

34. "Management of Negroes," *DeBow's Review* 11 (July–December 1851): 371. Robert Collins, "Management of Slaves," *DeBow's Review* 17 (July–December 1854): 424.

35. Collins, "Management of Slaves," 424.

36. "Management of Negroes upon Southern Estates," *DeBow's Review* 10 (January–June 1851): 625.

37. George Rawick, *Texas Narratives,* vol. 4 of *American Slave* (Westport, Conn.: Greenwood Press, 1972), suppl. 2, pt. 3, p. 370.

38. William B. Smith, "The Persimmon Tree and the Beer Dance," *Farmers Register* 6 (April 1838): 58–61.

39. Isaac D. Williams, *Sunshine and Shadow of Slave Life: Reminiscences as Told by Isaac D. Williams to "Tege"* (East Saginaw, Mich.: Evening News Printing and Binding House, 1885), 62.

40. George Rawick, *Mississippi Narrative,* vol. 9 of *American Slave* (Westport, Conn.: Greenwood Press, 1972), suppl. 1, pt. 4, p. 1418.

41. Interview with Foday Musa Suso, Mandingo griot, musician, and kora master, Providence, Rhode Island, October 29, 1986.

42. Federal Writers Project, WPA, *Texas,* vol. 16 of *Slave Narratives,* pt. 4 (Westport, Conn.: Greenwood Press, 1972).

43. Frederick Douglass, *Life and Times of Frederick Douglass* (London: Collier-Macmillan, 1961), 147.

44. Peter Wood, *Black Majority* (New York: Alfred A. Knopf, 1974).

45. *Statutes at Large for the State of South Carolina VII,* 410.

46. Robert Dirks, "Slaves' Holiday," *Natural History* 84, no. 10 (December 1975): 88. In late June 1835, several rumors circulated in Madison County, Mississippi, that a slave revolt was to commence; the date was uncertain, but there were two possibilities. One set of rumors confirmed Christmas Day 1835 as the appointed time. Prompted by the discovery of a plot in early 1709 in Surry, James City, and Isle of Wright counties, Virginia, the aroused whites seized and tortured several suspected slaves. Under torture, they admitted that a revolt had been planned for July 4, a holiday, "at which time it was felt that the slaves could assemble without suspicion" (Edwin A. Miles, "The Mississippi Slave Insurrection Scare of 1835," *Journal of Negro History* 42 [1957]: 49, 50). H. R. McIlwaine, ed., *Executive Journals of the Councils of Colonial Virginia* 3 (May 1, 1705–October 23, 1971): 234–35, 236. See also Herbert

Aptheker, *American Negro Slave Revolts* (New York: International Publishers, 1969), 169. Lieutenant Governor Jenings of Virginia issued a proclamation "to prevent negro slaves assembling together" (Cecil Headlam, *Calendar of State Papers, Colonial Series, America and West Indies: 1710–1711* 25 [London: 1960]: 238). Despite the proclamation, another well-developed plot was discovered in April 1709, again in Surry and James City counties. Lieutenant Governor Jenings's letter to the Council of Trade and Plantations dated April 24, 1710, illustrated the significance of holiday dances to the slave community: "there hath of late been very happily discovered an intended insurrection of the negroes, which was to have been put into execution in Surry and James City Countys on Easter Day; but the Chief conspirators having been seasonably apprehended, their design is broke" (Headlam, *Calendar,* 83).

47. An account of such a gathering is given in a letter written from Charleston, South Carolina, dated October 22, 1720:

> I shall give an account of a bloody tragedy which was to have been executed here last Saturday night (the 15th) by the Negroes, who had conspired to rise and destroy us and had almost bro't it to pass: but it pleased God to appear for us, and confound their Councils. For some of them propos'd that the Negroes of every Plantation should destroy their own Masters; but others were for rising in a Body, and giving the blow at once on surprise; and thus they differ's. They soon made a great Body at the back of the Town, and had a great Dance, and expected the Country Negroes to come &join them; and had not an overruling Providence discovered their Intrigues, we had been all in blood. For take the whole Province, we have about 28 thousand Negroes, to 3 thousand Whites. The Chief of them, with some others, is apprehended and in irons, in order to a tryal; and we are in Hopes to find out the whole affair (*Boston Weekly Newsletter,* October 15–22, 1730).

48. Edwin C. Holland, *A Refutation of the Calumnies Circulated Against the Southern and Eastern States* (Charleston: A. E. Miller, 1822), 59, 70, in Cornell University Rare Book Collection. The full passage on the 1730 incident is:

> One, that the negroes in each family in the dead of night, were to murder all their masters and the white men of every family, in the neighborhood in which there were no Negroes. *There was so much distrust and want of confidence,* however, among them that they resolved to adopt the other proposition, which was, they should assemble in the neighborhood of the town, under the pretense of a "Dancing Bout" and when proper preparations were made, to rush into the heart of the city, take possession of all arms and ammunition they could find, and murder all the white men, and then turn their forces to the different plantations.

49. General Oglethorpe to the accountant Mr. Harman Verelst, October 9, 1937, in Candler, comp. *Colonial Record* (Georgia), vol. 22, pt. 2 (Atlanta: Franklin Printing and Publishing Co., 1904–1918): 235. See also Epstein, *Sinful Tunes,* 40, 44. For examples of the drum used to call or signal a meeting or dance, see George W. Cable, "The Dance in Place Congo," *Century Magazine* 31 (April 1886): 517, and Georgia Writers Project, *Drums and Shadows,* 174.

50. A clear example of such paranoia at work is the case of the "New York Negro Plot of 1741." Suspects in the plot were slaves, soldiers, a Catholic priest, and several other whites. The paranoia resulted in the execution of thirty-one slaves, thirteen by burning, and eighteen by hanging. Seventy slaves were banished and four whites, including a Catholic priest (Aptheker, *Slave Revolts,* 193–95). Testimony given at the trial of the alleged conspirators stated that the plot was discussed at the tavern home of one Mr. Hughson, both at night and on Sunday, which was a slave holiday (Walter Prince, "New York Negro Plot of 1741," in

Saturday Chronicle, June 28–August 23, 1902, p. 31).
Other testimony claimed the details of the conspiracy were
negotiated at Christmastime, New Year's, and even Whitsuntide (ibid., 52–53). A well-known conspiracy that
emerged in Henrico County, Virginia, in 1800, set Saturday
as the day for the insurrection to occur. The chosen leader
of the rebels, Gabriel Prosser, used Sundays as a time to
gather information. Finally, Saturday, August 10, was set
for the rebellion (Aptheker, *Slave Revolts,* 221–22). Another example illustrates the significance of the holiday
dances: "Saturday Dec. 21—A court of Magistrates has
been sitting for the examination of two suspicious negroes.
One of them is said to have confessed being engaged
in a Scheme of insurrection to be put into execution at
Christmas time" (Sherwin McRae, ed., *Calendar of Virginia State Papers* 9 [Richmond, Va.: Thomas Matthews,
1890]: 309).

51. Richard C. Wade, *Slavery in the Cities* (New York:
Oxford University Press, 1964), 48–54, 55–59. See also
August Meier and Elliott M. Rudwick, *From Plantation to
Ghetto* (New York: Hill and Wang, 1866), 66. On view of
urban slaves, see Farley Reynolds, "The Urbanization of
Negroes in the United States," *Journal of Social History* 1
(Spring 1968): 246, and Marion deB. Kilson, "Towards
Freedom: An Analysis of Slave Revolts in the United
States," *Phylon* 25 (Summer 1964): 176.

52. A letter to the *South Carolina Gazette* in 1772 re-
veals what was probably a typical occurrence of the time
regarding the control of urban slaves:

> Whoever may please to walk or ride, from this town,
> only so far as where the road divides near the Quarter-
> House, from about 3 hours before sun setting on Satur-
> day afternoon, till 11 o'clock at night, and from about
> two hours before sun-rising till an hour after it sets on
> Sunday, will not be long at a loss to answer the question:
> For tho' he will find the numbers passing and repassing

between these periods never to be less than *four hundred*, but often exceeding seven yet he will rarely meet with more than 40 or 50 tickets or letters in the hands of the *Country Negroes* and never more than 4 or 5 such [licences] among those that belong to the Town, who generally make four-fifths of these strollers (*South Carolina Gazette,* September 17, 1772).

53. Ibid. For a more complete description of runaways in cities, see Wade, *Slavery in Cities,* 209–25.

54. Le Page du Pratz, A. S., *History of Louisiana* (Baton Rouge: Louisiana State University Press, 1975), 380, 384, 387.

55. Henry A. Kmen, *Music in New Orleans* (Baton Rouge: Louisiana State University Press, 1966), 226–27; Christian Schultz, *Travels on an Inland Voyage . . . ,* vol. 2 (New York, 1810), 197. For a discussion that views Congo Square as a means to encourage slave dancing, see John Blassingame, *The Slave Community,* rev. ed. (New York: Oxford University Press, 1979), 36.

56. Russell R. Menard, "The Maryland Slave Population, 1658 to 1730: A Demographic Profile of Blacks in Four Counties," *William and Mary Quarterly,* 3rd ser. 32 (January 1975): 29–54. John Mason Peck, *Forty Years of Pioneer Life,* ed. Rufus Babcock (Philadelphia: American Baptist Publication Society, c. 1864): 90.

57. Harriet Brent Jacobs, *Incidents in the Life of a Slave Girl* (Boston: 1861), 179–81.

58. Ira DE A. Reid, "The John Canoe Festival," *Phylon* 3 (4): 350, 356. See also Dougald MacMillan, "John Kuners," *Journal of American Folklore* 39 (January–March 1926): 53–57; Frederic G. Cassidy, "Hipsaw and John Canoe," *American Speech* 41 (February 1966): 45–51; and "Slaves Holiday," *Natural History* 84, no. 10 (December 1975): 82–89. For descriptions of Dia de Reyes, see Fernanto Ortiz, *Los Bailes y el Teatro de los Negros en el Folklore de Cuba* (Habana: Ediciones Cardenas y Cia,

1951), and Ortiz, "La Fiesta Afrocubano del 'Dia de Reyes,'" *Extracto de los Archivas del Folklore Cubano* 1, no. 17 (1925). For a description of John Canoe dancing and festivities in Jamaica, see Margaret Shedd, "Carib Dance Patterns," *Theatre Arts Monthly* 17, no. 1 (January 1933): 65–77.

59. Edwin Olson, "Social Aspects of Slave Life in New York," *Journal of Negro History* 26 (January 1941): 66–77.

60. George Rogers Howell, *Bicentennial History of Albany. History of the County of Albany, N.Y., from 1609 to 1886* (New York: W. W. Munsell, 1886), 725. Mary Gay Humphreys, *Catherine Schuyler* (New York: Charles Scribner's Sons, 1897), 39.

61. Herbert S. Aimes, "African Institutions in America," *Journal of American Folk-Lore* 18 (1905): 15.

62. Joseph P. Reidy, "'Negro Election Day' and Black Community Life in New England, 1750–1860," *Marxist Perspectives* (Fall 1978): 102. Orville H. Platt, "Negro Governors," *Papers of the New Haven Colonial Historical Society* 6 (1900): 335.

63. Aimes, "African Institutions," 16.

64. Fisk University, *Unwritten History of Slavery* (Nashville: Social Science Institute, 1945), 50.

65. "Corn Shuckin' Down South," *New York Sun,* November 11, 1895, p. 4. See also George Wiley, M.D., *Southern Plantation Stories and Sketches* (Freeport, N.Y.: Books for Libraries Press, 1971), 41–52.

66. David C. Barrow, Jr., "A Georgia Corn-Shucking," *Century Magazine* 24 (May–October 1882): 878. William Cullen Bryant, "Southern Negro Life," *DeBow's Review* 9 (1850): 325–27.

67. Barrow, "Georgia Corn-Shucking," 878.

68. Genovese, *Roll Jordan Roll,* 318.

69. Bertram Doyle, *The Etiquette of Race Relations in the South* (Port Washington, N.Y.: Kennikat Press, 1968), 22–23. Robert Farris Thompson, "An Aesthetic of the

Cool: West African Dance," *African Forum* 2 (Fall 1966): 96; see also Camille Poupeye, "Danses dramatiques en théâtres exotiques," *Les Cahiers du Journal des Poètes* (Brussels, 1941): 109. This phenomenon has also been observed among Puerto Ricans in New York City.

70. Rudi Blesh and Harriet Janis, *They All Played Ragtime* (New York: Alfred A. Knopf, 1950), 96.

71. *South Carolina Gazette,* September 17, 1772.

72. Samuel Mordecai, *Virginia, Especially Richmond* (Richmond: West & Johnston, 1860), 351–55, 357.

73. *DeBow's Review* 27 (May 1853): 573; see also Nehemiah Adams, *South Side View of Slavery,* 1969, 29.

74. Urlich Bonnell Phillips, *American Negro Slavery* (New York: D. Appleton and Company, 1918), 415.

75. Eyre Crowe, *With Thackeray in America* (New York: Charles Scribner's Sons, 1893), 147–48.

76. Frederick Law Olmsted, *A Journey in the Seaboard Slave states,* vol. 2 (New York: G. P. Putnam's Sons, 1904), See also Montgomery, Alabama City Records, December 1856.

77. Federal Writers Project, WPA *Georgia,* vol. 4 of *Slave Narratives,* pt. 4 (Westport, Conn.: Greenwood Press, 1972), p. 224.

78. "The Quadroons of Louisiana," unpublished manuscript, in Charles E. A. Gayarre Collection, Department of Archives and Manuscript, Louisiana State University, Baton Rouge, 2.

79. Ibid.

80. See Haramannus Hoetink, *Slavery; and Race Relations in the Americas* (New York: Harper & Row, 1973), 12, 30; see also Hoetink, "Surinam and Curacao," in *Neither Slave nor Free,* ed. David Cohen and Jack P. Green (Baltimore: Johns Hopkins University Press, 1972), 61.

81. Thomas Cottle, "Social Class and Social Dancing," *Sociological Quarterly* 7 (Spring 1966): 179. The terms

mulatto, quadroon, and *octoroon* were part of an extensive nomenclature developed to classify slaves and people of African descent. Most slave merchants and owners were familiar with some system of classification; however, the system used by the French reflects a peculiarly elaborate typology. These three terms, plus *sang mele, maraboun, meamolouc,* and *griffe,* came into use to distinguish a class of persons whose parentage was both black and white. These terms reflect the social distinction between whites, coloreds, and blacks that existed under Spanish and French slavery. In Barbados supper dances were often organized by free colored hotel-tavern proprietresses; see Gerome I. Handler and Charlotte G. Frisbie, "Aspects of Slave Life in Barbados: Music and Its Cultural Context," *Caribbean Studies* 2, no. 4 (January 1972): 39. For a description of quadroon balls and women, see Grace King, *New Orleans: The Place and the People* (New York: Macmillan, 1895), 344–45, 349–50; also Olmsted, *Journey,* 594–97; Edward Byron Reuter, *Race Mixture* (New York: McGraw-Hill, 1931), 40–47; Annie Lee West Stahl, "The Free Negro in Ante-Bellum Louisiana" (unpublished thesis, Louisiana State University, 1934); Harriet Martineau, *Society in America,* vol. 2 (Paris: 1837), 116–17; Herbert Asbury, *The French Quarter* (New York: Garden City Publishing, 1938), 128–35; Donald E. Everett, "Free People of Color in New Orleans, 1803–1865" (unpublished dissertation, Tulane University, 1952), 33, 36, 190, 264–66; and "Quadroons of Louisiana," 2.

82. "Quadroons of Louisiana," 3; see also Eliza Potter, *A Hairdresser's Experience in High Life* (Cincinnati, Ohio: privately published, 1859), 22, 254, 188–90.

83. See "Alphabetical and Chronological Digest of the Acts and Deliberations of the Cabildo, 1769–1803: A Record of the Spanish Government in New Orleans," comp. and ed. Works Progress Administration, New Orleans, 1939

(typescript in City Archives, New Orleans Public Library), quoted in Everett, "Free People," 40. The play *The Octoroon: Or Life in Louisiana,* by Dion Boucicault (London: J. Dicks, 1862), tells the story of an octoroon girl, the daughter of a wealthy white judge and his quadroon housekeeper. The judge has freed his daughter from slavery, but after his death she is sold into servitude to pay his debts. Of course, the realities of this dramatization were not frequent; it merely serves to demonstrate the tenuous position of these *gens de couleur.* For a true-to-life example, see John W. Coleman, Jr., *Slavery Times in Kentucky* (Chapel Hill: University of North Carolina Press, 1940).

84. "Quadroons of Louisiana," 2. "Acts Passed at the First Session of the First Legislature of the Territory of Orleans" (1806), 188; quoted in Everett, "Free People," 167.

85. "Quadroons of Louisiana," 4–5; see also King, *New Orleans,* 347–58, and Lyle Saxon, *Fabulous New Orleans* (New Orleans: Robert L. Crager, 1950), 180.

86. Roger A. Fischer, "Racial Segregation in Ante-Bellum New Orleans," *American Historical Review* 74 (February 1969): 933. *Documents of the Cabildo,* Louisiana State Museum Library, New Orleans, book 4088, document 338.

87. Henry A. Kmen, *Music in New Orleans* (Baton Rouge: Louisiana State University Press), 43–44.

88. Ibid., 46, 45.

89. Berquin-Duvallon, *Vue de la Colonie Espagnole du Mississippi ou des Provinces de Louisiane et Floride Occidentale, en l'Anné 1802* (Paris: 1803), 185–86.

90. Kmen, *Music in New Orleans,* 47. "Racial Segregation in New Orleans," 935.

91. Albert Phelps, *Louisiana* (New York: Houghton, Mifflin, 1905), 212.

92. Asbury, *French Quarter,* 134; Bernard, Duke of Saxe-Weimer Eisenach, "Travels through North America

during the Years of 1825 and 1827," in *Journal of Negro History* 2 (January 1917): 177–81.

93. Olmsted, *Journey,* 598–602. Arthur W. Calhoun, *A Social History of the American Family,* vol. 1 (Cleveland: 1971), 331, quoted in E. Franklin Frazier, *The Free Negro Family: A Study of Family Origins before the Civil War* (Nashville, Tenn.: Fisk University Press, 1932), 29. See also Laura Foner, "The People of Color in Louisiana and St. Dominique," *Journal of Social History* 3 (Summer 1970): 408; Edward B. Reuter, *The Mulatto in the United States* (Boston: Gorham Press, 1918), 91, 378. Genovese, *Roll Jordan Roll,* 417–18; and Joe M. Richardson, "A Negro Success Story: James Dallas Burrus," *Journal of Negro History* 50 (October 1965): 274.

94. Saxon, *Fabulous New Orleans,* 180. See also Foner, "People of Color," 409; Joe Gray Taylor, *Negro Slavery in Louisiana* (Baton Rouge: Louisiana Historical Association, 1963), 162–65; and Sister Frances Jerome Woods, C.D.P., *Marginality and Identity* (Baton Rouge: Louisiana State University Press, 1972), 30.

95. Pierre Paul Ebeyer, *Paramours of the Creoles* (New Orleans: Windmill Publishing, 1945), 33; see also W. Adolphe Roberts, *Lake Pontchartrain* (Indianapolis: Bobbs Merrill, 1946), 143; Asbury, *French Quarter,* 134; King, *New Orleans,* 347; "Quadroons of Louisiana," 16; Bernard, Duke of Saxe Weimar Eisenach, "Travels through North America"; and George W. Cable, "Creole Slave Songs," *Century Magazine* 31 (April 1886): 808.

96. Asbury, *French Quarter,* 131. Foner, "People of Color," 41; Laura Robinson, *It's an Old New Orleans Custom* (New York: Vanguard Press, 1948), 219. Edward Larocque Tinker, *Creole City* (New York: Longmans, Green, 1953), 260. Olmsted, quoted in Roberts, *Lake Pontchartrain,* 146. Bernard, Duke of Saxe-Weimar Eisenach, "Travels through North America," 57–59. John Winston Coleman, Jr., *Slavery Times in Kentucky* (Chapel Hill: University of

North Carolina Press, 1940), 158–59. This procedure differed from the "fancy girl" markets of Lexington, Louisville, or New Orleans (the best known and largest). These markets specialized in beautiful, shapely, and usually lighter colored women, who in all probability, could become the mistress of their purchaser. The quadroon balls probably provided the "fancy girl" marketeers with their biggest source of competition. And it is not unlikely that slave traders took their "fancy girls" to the quadroon balls as well.

97. For comments on the frequency of these balls see *New Orleans Daily Picayune,* May 24, 1849; Advertisements in this issue indicated that quadroon balls were held at the Louisiana Ball Room on Thursday, Friday, and Saturday nights. Stephen Longstreet, *Sportin' House* (Los Angeles: Sherbourne Press, 1965), states that there were eight to twelve balls per month (p. 111). H. E. Sterks, *The Free Negro in Ante-Bellum Louisiana* (Teaneck, N.J.: Fairleigh Dickinson University Press, 1972), 61–62; see also Charles Etienne Gayarre, *History of Louisiana,* vol. 3, p. 179. For the 1828 ordinance, see Fischer, "Racial Segregation in New Orleans," 935.

98. Robert C. Reinders, "The Decline of the New Orleans Free Negroes in the Decade Before the Civil War," *Journal of Mississippi History* 24 (April 1962): 88–89. For a discussion of the role of the press in the decline of status of blacks in the 1850s, see Lawrence Dunbar Reddick, "The Negro in the New Orleans Press, 1850–1869: A Study in Attitudes and Propaganda" (unpublished dissertation, University of Chicago, 1939). *Daily Picayune,* November 3, 1860, and March 15, 1859, quoted in Reinders, "Decline of New Orleans Negroes," 91. Sterks, *Free Negro,* 299, 300.

99. Asbury, *French Quarter,* 134. According to Asbury, by 1850 New Orleans was rapidly becoming Americanized; the city of almost 125,000 "had simply outgrown such exotic displays."

CHAPTER TWO

1. Peter Kolchin, *First Freedom* (Westport, Conn.: Greenwood Press, 1972); this process of migration away from the rural areas and into the southern urban centers is described in detail.

2. Fisk University, *God Struck Me Dead: Religious Conversion Experiences and Autobiographies of Negro Ex-Slaves* (Nashville, Tenn.: Social Science Institute, 1945), 177; see also Fisk University, *Unwritten History of Slavery: Autobiographical Accounts of Negro Ex-Slaves* (Nashville, Tenn.: Social Science Institute, 1945), 256. Thomas Webber, *Deep Like the Rivers* (New York: W. W. Norton, 1978), 143, 232–33.

3. Webber, *Deep Like the Rivers,* 224–43; Webber has an entire chapter examining the community, and the phenomenon of community orientation. Paul Escott, *Slavery Remembered* (Chapel Hill: University of North Carolina Press, 1979), 96; Escott gives three primary reasons for the solidarity and power of slave culture, one being the common bond of enslavement. John Blassingame, *The Slave Community,* rev. ed. (New York: Oxford University Press, 1979), 315–16.

4. Charles C. Jones, *The Religious Instruction of the Negroes in the United States* (Savannah, Ga.: 1842), 130–31.

5. Frederick Douglass, *My Bondage and My Freedom* (New York: 1855), 55.

6. Robert Farris Thompson, *Flash of the Spirit* (New York: Random House, 1983), 237. See also Lydia Cabrera, *La Sociedad Secreta Abakuá,* (Miami, Fla.: Coleccion del Chicherekú, 1970).

7. Kolchin, *First Freedom,* 36, 52, 53. W. E. B. DuBois, *Black Reconstruction* (Cleveland: World Publishing, 1935), 134–35, 169–71, 177–79, 458. *Selma Morning Times,* December 9, 1865.

8. Marshall and Jean Stearns, *Jazz Dance* (New York: Macmillan, 1968), 71–72.

9. Richard W. Thomas, "Working Class Origins of Black Culture: Class Formation and the Division of Black Cultural Labor," *Minority Voices* 1, (Fall 1977): 88–89. The most important early organizations formed by African-Americans in the urban North were the secret societies and voluntary fraternal lodges described earlier. In many cities these organizations predated emancipation. In Boston, the Prince Hall Masons were established by the 1870s and by 1885 there were fifteen Masonic lodges in Chicago. The Odd Fellows had six chapters in Chicago by the 1880s. In Cleveland the Masons dated back to 1800, the Elks were established by 1880, and the Odd Fellows established their first chapter in 1856. Black Masonry reached Michigan by 1859, and in 1864 the first Detroit lodge was organized, followed by a second lodge in 1869. The Odd Fellows made their first appearance in Detroit in 1885. The Elks formed its first Detroit chapter in 1905. The Knights of Pythias, United Brothers of Friendship, Good Samaritans, and True Reformers began to appear in Detroit in the 1890s. In New York City the best known of the fraternal orders were sufficiently well established to move from downtown to new Harlem quarters by the early 1920s. These included the United Order of True Reformers, Odd Fellows, Masons, Elks, and the Knights of Pythias. For a detailed history of black benevolent societies see Edward N. Palmer, "Negro Secret Societies," *Social Forces* 23 (December 1944): 207–12; Charles W. Ferguson, *Fifty Million Brothers: A Panorama of American Lodges and Clubs* (New York: Farrar and Rinehart, 1937), chap. 13; Charles H. Brooks, *A History and Manual of the Grand United Order of Odd Fellows in America* (Philadelphia: Odd Fellows Journal Print, 1902); Charles H. Wesley, *The History of the Prince Hall Grand Lodge of Free and Accepted Masons of the State of Ohio* (Wilberforce, Ohio: Central State College Press,

1961); and E. A. Williams, *History and Manual of the Colored Knights of Pythias* (Nashville, Tenn.: Nashville Baptist Publishing Board, 1917).

10. Monroe N. Work, "Secret Societies As Factors in the Social and Economical Life of The Negro," in *Democracy in Earnest,* ed. James McColloch (Southern Sociological Congress, 1918), 343–47. It is estimated that free African-Americans formed mutual aid organizations as far back as 1820. In Lexington, Kentucky, the Union Benevolent Society was established in 1843, and in 1852 it organized a lodge among slaves. In Montgomery, Alabama, slaves formed clubs that gave social affairs and saw to the numerous needs of its members (see City Council records of Montgomery, Alabama, December, 1856).

11. Thomas, "Working Class Origins," 91. See *Black Republican,* April 15, 1865: benefit fair and musical soirée to be held on May 13, 1865 advertised as "benefits for orphans of freedman and in aid of Soule House, a Colored Orphan Home." For a comprehensive listing of African-American educational institutions, see William N. Hartshorn, ed., *An Era of Progress and Promise, 1863–1910* (Boston: Priscilla Publishing, 1910).

12. John W. Blassingame, *Black New Orleans, 1860–1880* (Chicago: University of Chicago Press, 1973), 145–46. For a discussion of social differentiation in the slave community, see John W. Blassingame, "Social Structure in the Slave Community: Evidence from New Sources," in *Perspectives and Irony in American Slavery,* ed. Harry Owens (Jackson: University Press of Mississippi, 1976), 137–51. See Samuel Mordecai, *Virginia Especially Richmond in By-Gone Days* (Richmond: West & Johnston, 1860); the section entitled "The Colored Aristocracy" (p. 350) gives an excellent description of how labor served to differentiate slaves.

13. *Cleveland Gazette,* August 21, 1886. William H. Wiggins, Jr., "'Lift Every Voice': A Study of Afro-American

Emancipation Celebrations," in *Discovering Afro-America,* ed. Roger D. Abrahams and John F. Szwed (The Netherlands: E. J. Brill-Leiden, 1975), 46–57. Other celebrations like the January 1 "day of days" had religious overtones. January 1 and February 1 celebrations were based on the rituals of the African-American church; in contrast to the all-day secular celebrations, these affairs took several hours and were held in black churches. For a good account of January 1 celebrations, see William H. Wiggins, Jr., "January 1: The Afro-American's 'Day of Days,'" in *Prospects: An Annual of American Cultural Studies,* ed. Jack Salzman, vol. 4 (New York: Burt Franklin & Co., 1979), 331–54.

14. Wiggins, "Lift Every Voice."

15. Wendy Watriss, "Celebrate Freedom: Juneteenth," *Southern Exposure* 5 (1): 80. William H. Wiggins, Jr., "Juneteenth," *American Vision,* June 1986, p. 41. *Juneteenth: Celebrating Emancipation* (program pamphlet of the National Museum of American History, Smithsonian Institution, Washington, D.C., June 8, 1985), 7.

16. Wiggins, "January 1," 346. Wiggins, "Lift Every Voice," 188; for additional information on Juneteenth, see Michael Point, "Juneteenth Blues Festival," *Downbeat* 49 (November 1982): 57; *Sepia* 31, no. 1 (June 1982): 78; "Juneteenth Becomes State Holiday in Texas," *Jet* 56, no. 1 (July 19, 1979): 8; Don Shirley, "Juneteenth," Los Angeles Cultural Center pamphlet, vol. 102, sec. VI (October 7, 1983), p. 2.

17. DuBois, *Black Reconstruction,* 670–709; throughout, DuBois gives detailed descriptions and numerous examples of the kind of mob violence used to terrorize African-Americans. Also see Kenneth Kusmer, *A Ghetto Takes Shape: Black Cleveland 1870–1930* (Urbana: University of Illinois Press, 1976), 158–60; Charles H. Wesley, *Negro Labor in the United States, 1850–1925: A Study in American Economic History* (New York: Vanguard Press, 1927), 290–92; Louise Venable Kennedy, *The Negro Peasant*

Turns Cityward (New York: Columbia University Press, 1930), 42–48; Emmett J. Scott, *Negro Migration During the War* (New York: Arno Press, 1920), 13–15 and *passim;* George Edmund Haynes, "Negroes Move North," *Survey* 40 (May 4, 1918): 115–22; Florette Henri, *Black Migration: Movement North, 1900–1920* (New York: Doubleday, 1976), 47–62; and Russell Davis, *Black Americans in Cleveland: From George Peake to Carl B. Stokes, 1796–1969* (Washington, D.C.: Associated Publishers, 1972), 129.

18. Carol A. Stroman, "The Chicago Defender and the Mass Migration of Blacks, 1916–1918," *Journal of Popular Culture* 15 (Fall 1981): 62–67.

19. Kusmer, *A Ghetto Takes Shape,* 96–98; David Katzman, *Before the Ghetto* (Urbana: University of Illinois Press, 1973), 150–51; Allan H. Spear, *Black Chicago,* (Chicago: The University of Chicago Press, 1967), 107–9. See also lodge notices in black newspapers for respective cities, *Cleveland Gazette,* 1890–1915, and *Cleveland Journal,* 1903–1910. In Cleveland a second Odd Fellows Lodge was organized in 1892. In 1868 the Ruth Degree, an organization of Odd Fellow wives, sisters, daughters, and mothers, was opened. Several other groups, military in nature, were organized and gave dances, but they were short-lived. See Davis, *Black Americans in Cleveland,* 124. See also John H. Taitt, *The Souvenir of Negro Progress: Chicago, 1779–1925* (Chicago: DeSaible Association, 1925) [n.p.]; *Appeal,* February 27, 1892; *Defender,* January 27, 1912; St. Clair Drake and Horace Cayton, *Black Metropolis* (New York: Harcourt, Brace & Company, 1945), vol. 1, 54, 145–46.

20. Katzman, *Before the Ghetto,* 147–53. For accounts of upper-strata black life in Boston, see Adelaide Cromwell Hill, "The Negro Upper Class in Boston—Its Development and Present Social Structure" (unpublished dissertation, Radcliff College, 1952).

21. Interview with Arrie Jenkins Jones, black socialite, Cleveland, November 9, 1979.

22. *Cleveland Gazette,* April 14, 1917. Description of "after Lenten dance" reads: "One of the most delightful affairs of the season took place Monday evening at Dreamland when under the auspices of the Men's Club of St. Andrews Church, society gathered for its after Lenten dance. There were 400 in attendance and the affair was a most satisfactory success."

23. Jones interview.

24. Eugene Genovese, *Roll Jordan Roll* (New York: Random House, 1976), 570–71. C. Vann Woodward, *Origins of the New South, 1877–1913* (Baton Rouge: Louisiana State University Press, 1951). Also see Blassingame *Slave Community,* 43–44; William Webb, *The History of William Webb* (Detroit: E. Hoekstra, printer, 1873), 8–12.

25. Sandra R. Lieb, *Mother of the Blues: A Study of Ma Rainey* (Amherst: University of Massachusetts Press, 1981), 28. Dorsey served as Ma Rainey's accompanist and band director, assembling the Wildcat Jazz Band.

26. Federal Writers Project, WPA, *Texas Narratives,* vol. 16 of *Slave Narratives,* pt. 4 (Westport, Conn.: Greenwood Press, 1972), p. 198.

27. Zora Neal Hurston, "Characteristics of Negro Expression," in *Negro Anthology,* ed. Nancy Cunard (New York: Negro Universities Press, 1969), 44. Johnny Shines, quoted in Giles Oakley, *The Devil's Music* (New York: Harcourt, Brace, Jovanovich, 1976), 214.

28. Lorenzo D. Turner, *Africanisms in the Gullah Dialect* (Chicago: University of Chicago Press, 1959), 195. Correspondence with Robert Farris Thompson, January 29, 1985.

29. John S. Otto and Augustus M. Burns, "Black and White Cultural Interaction in the Early Twentieth Century South: Race and Hillbilly Music," *Phylon* 24 (December 1974): 413. LeRoi Jones, *Blues People: Negro Music in*

White America (New York: Morrow, 1963), 64–65; see also Kolchin, *First Freedom,* 36, 52, passim; and Henri, *Black Migration,* 27.

30. Hurston, "Characteristics," p. 44, uses the description "shoddy confines." In the jook, an increased flow of new material influenced the development of the already standardized dances. "The Negro dances circulated over the world were also conceived inside the jooks. They too make the rounds of jooks and public works before going into the outside world" (Hurston, "Characteristics," 44).

31. For accounts of the "ring shout," see Charlotte Forten, *The Journal of Charlotte Forten,* ed. Ray Allen Billington (New York: W. W. Norton, 1981), 166, 175, 180, 184, 205, 206, 209, 212, and 224. See also Thomas Wentworth Higginson, *Army Life in a Black Regiment* (Boston: Fields, Osgood, 1870), 17, 24, 197–98; Lydia Parrish, *Slave Songs of the Georgia Sea Islands* (New York: Creative Age Press, 1942), 54–55; and James McPherson, *The Negro's Civil War* (New York: Vintage Books, 1965).

32. Otto and Burns, "Black and White Interaction," 413.

33. Hurston, "Characteristics," p. 44.

34. Musician Johnny Shines comments: "When you are playing in a place like that, you just sit there on the floor in a cane-bottom chair, just rear back and cut loose. There were no microphones or P.A. set ups there; you just sing out as loud as you can" (Oakley, *Devil's Music,* 214).

35. Hurston, "Characteristics," 44. Marshall and Jean Stearns, *Jazz Dance* (New York: Macmillan, 1968), 23–24; see also Parrish, *Slave Songs,* 128, 145; Georgia Writers Project, WPA, *Drums and Shadows* (Athens: University of Georgia Press, 1940), 115.

36. Dances involving scratching, as if to relieve an itching sensation, can be observed in numerous African groups as well as among New World Africans and their descendents. In West Africa these dances were originally to

the deity that controlled sickness and disease. Among the Nigerian Yoruba he is known as Sopona, the deity controlling smallpox. His New World names include Obaluaye, Babaluaye, and St. Lazarus. Here the African-American custom of spitting on the broom—if one's feet are accidentally swept—may be related to Sopona/Obaluaye, who appears clothed in straw and raffia (Stearns, *Jazz Dance*, 27).

37. Interview with Riley "B. B." King, blues singer, Ithaca, New York, March 1981. Mr. King comments on the size of the average jook: "Most places could hold forty or fifty people; some of the really big places could hold up to one hundred and fifty."

38. *The Saga of Mr. Jelly Lord*, vol. 5, Library of Congress audio recording. Ibid., vol. 12.

39. Alan Lomax, *Mr. Jelly Roll* (New York: Duell, Sloan and Pearce, 1950), 58.

40. Hortense Powdermaker, *After Freedom, A Cultural Study of the Deep South* (New York: Viking Press, 1939), 8; see also E. Franklin Frazier, "Recreation and Amusement Among American Negroes" (Research monograph, July 15, 1940), 22–23.

41. Charles Keil, *Urban Blues* (Chicago: University of Chicago Press, 1966), 54–55. Donald Marquis, *In Search of Buddy Bolden* (New York: DaCapo Press, 1978), 58.

42. Stearns, *Jazz Dance*, 110.

43. Chadwick Hansen, "Jenny's Toe: Negro Shaking Dances," *American Quarterly* 19 (3): 561. The same leg gesture can be observed in certain dances in Sierra Leone, West Africa.

44. From interview with Mrs. Leola Wilson (Coot Grant), Whitesboro, New Jersey, 1959–60, in Stearns, *Jazz Dance*, 24.

45. Stearns, *Jazz Dance*, 21–23. Cornetist Charlie Love, born in 1885, who played for dances around the turn of the century, comments: "Eagle Rock, the Buzzard Lope, and the Slow Drag were the favorite dances. They did the

Slow Drag all over Louisiana . . . couples would hang onto each other and just grind back and forth in one spot all night" (21–23).

46. Interview with George Gould, former vaudeville entertainer, Cleveland, Ohio, 1979.

47. Interview with Walter Carroll, jukebox salesman and company owner, Cleveland, Ohio, 1979.

48. Chris Albertson, *Bessie* (New York: Stein and Day, 1974), 122.

49. Perry Bradford, *Born with the Blues* (New York: Oak Publications, 1965), 163–64.

50. For an explanation of the various ways that numbers were played, see Drake and Cayton, *Black Metropolis,* vol. 2, 470–94; see also J. Saunders Redding, "Playing the Numbers," *North American Review* 238 (December 1934): 533–42. On political relationships, see Bradford, *Born with the Blues,* 164.

51. Zora Neal Hurston, *Mules and Men* (New York: Harper and Row, 1970), 193–95. I recall going to an after-hours joint in the Central Avenue area of Cleveland, Ohio, in 1971, where all patrons were required to surrender their weapon at the door.

52. William Ferris, *Blues from the Delta* (New York: Doubleday, 1979), 21.

53. J. T. Woofter, *Negro Problems in Cities* (New York: Doubleday, Doran and Co., 1928), 29; see also Henri, *Black Migrations,* 51–102. The following synonyms for rent party were found: Rent shout, chittlin' shout, chittlin' strut, rent strut, Blue Monday party, chittlin' switch, house shout, and chittlin' rag were generally used in the South and Midwest. Parlor social, social whist party, social party, too-terrible party, too-bad party, matinee party, struggle, breakdown, razor drill, flopwallie, and chitterling party were used in both the South and in northeastern cities.

54. *Central Area Social Study* (Research committee of the Welfare Federation of Cleveland, March 1942–July

1944), 42, 85–102; see also Katzman, *Before the Ghetto,* 147, passim; Gilbert Osofsky, *Harlem* (New York: Harper and Row, 1965), 120, passim; and Spear, *Black Chicago,* 147–51. *Cleveland Call and Post,* November 8, 1941.

55. *Central Area Study,* 43–44. In 1939 a random sample of 10,604 family and nonfamily units was studied by the Real Property Inventory of Metropolitan Cleveland; 8,525 were white and 2,079 were black. The white group had a yearly median income of $960 compared with $641 for the black group. The white families paid a median rent of $19.08 per month and the black families $16.25 per month. In the twenty-five census tracts having 50 percent or more blacks, the median rent for substandard family units occupied by white tenant families was $17.28; the figure for black tenant families was $28.05, a difference of about 38 percent.

56. Ira DE A. Reid, "Mrs. Bailey Pays the Rent," in *The New Negro Renaissance,* ed. Arthur P. Davis and Michael W. Peplow (New York: Holt, Rinehart and Winston, 1957), 164–65. Osofsky, *Harlem,* 13, 136; see also Spear, *Black Chicago,* 23–25. Maurice Waller and Anthony Calabrese, *Fats Waller* (New York: Macmillan, 1977), 5.

57. Reid, "Mrs. Bailey," 167.

58. Gould interview. Christopher Wye, "The New Deal and the Negro Community," *Journal of American History* 59 (December 1972): 631. See also "Annual Report of the Negro Welfare Association, 1933," Cleveland Urban League Manuscript in Western Reserve Historical Society, Cleveland, Ohio.

59. Charles Jarmon, "The Sploe House: A Drinking Place of Lower Socio-Economic Status Negroes in a Southern City," *Black Experience: A Southern University Journal* 55 (June 1969): 53–61.

60. Reid, "Mrs. Bailey," Oakley, *Devil's Music,* 163.

61. Interview with Earl Royster, performer, November 1980, Boston; see also Wallace Thurman, *The Blacker the*

Berry (New York: Macmillan, 1970), 153; Reid, "Mrs. Bailey," 170–71.

62. Gould interview; see also Thurman, *Blacker the Berry,* 153.

63. Interview with Tito Cavalero, performer, December 1979, Cleveland, Ohio, also Gould interview; see also Waller and Calabrese, *Fats Waller,* 12; James Haskins, *Scott Joplin* (New York: Stein and Day, 1978), 120. Jarvice Anderson, *This Was Harlem* (New York: Farrar, Straus, Giroux, 1982), 154–55. Joel Vance, *Ain't Misbehavin'* (New York: Berkey Publishing, 1979), 44–45.

64. Thurman, *Blacker the Berry,* 152–53.

65. Reid, "Mrs. Bailey," 170. Interviews with jukebox company owners Walter Carroll and Buddy Crew, January 1980, Cleveland, Ohio.

66. Conversation with Mrs. Ozora James, born 1894, who gave numerous rent parties, December 1979, Cleveland, Ohio. Reid, "Mrs. Bailey," 166; Thurman, *Blacker the Berry,* 152.

67. Vance, *Ain't Misbehavin',* 44–45; see also Waller and Calabrese, *Fats Waller,* 30–31.

68. Clyde Vernon Kiser, *Sea Island to City* (New York: AMS Press, 1967), 45. Reid, "Mrs. Bailey," 168.

69. Reid, "Mrs. Bailey," 169.

70. Waller and Calabrese, *Fats Waller,* 30.

71. Oakley, *Devil's Music,* 163; also Gould interview. Wye, "New Deal," 621–39. *Cleveland Call and Post,* February 28, 1942. In Cleveland, for example, the large-scale evictions accelerated when a low-income housing project was built in the lower-west section of the Central area. Although this project was described as low-income housing and ostensibly eased the situation in the congested Central area, closer examination revealed that it intensified the overcrowding in the black community by tearing down 30,000 units of housing and building only 10,000, which were reserved for "white only." This only forced the dis-

placed families deeper into the ghetto and increased the density in the community.

72. Reid, "Mrs. Bailey," 164. On population density, see Woofter, *Negro Problems,* 29. In 1925 Woofter studied the conditions of rent in sixteen urban areas, seven of them in the North, nine in the South. In each city he examined the problems of high population density, congestion, and exploitation. In New York, Philadelphia, Chicago, Buffalo, Indianapolis, Gary, and Dayton, all black areas experienced a level of density greater than the white areas; consider the following figures:

City	Density per acre (white)	Density per acre (black)
New York	223	336
Philadelphia	28	111
Chicago	31	67
Buffalo	15	40
Indianapolis	15	21
Gary	5	21
Dayton	17	20

Woofter also found a higher percentage of black families with lodgers. Consider the following (figures for Chicago in 1925 were unavailable):

City	Families canvassed	Families with lodgers	Total no. of lodgers	% families with lodgers
New York	1,627	513	874	32
Philadelphia	2,531	948	2,438	37
Buffalo	53	26	62	49
Indianapolis	207	51	131	25
Gary	111	27	64	24
Dayton	231	64	178	28

73. Langston Hughes, "From the Big Sea," in *The New Negro Renaissance,* ed. Arthur P. Davis and Michael W. Peplow (New York: Holt Rinehart and Winston, 1975),

177. Not all rent parties were sponsored by needy migrants struggling to meet the rent. Some were given by African-American property owners looking to gain extra dollars. Others were given solely as alternatives to the tourist-invaded cabarets and clubs that catered to whites looking for black entertainment. Langston Hughes had this comment: "Then it was that house-rent parties began to flourish—and not always to raise the rent either. But, as often as not, to have a get-together of one's own, where you could do the black-bottom with no stranger behind you trying to do it too." Jarvis Anderson, *This Was Harlem* (New York: Farrar, Straus, Giroux, 1982), 154–55.

74. Maya Angelou, *Singing and Swinging and Getting Merry Like Christmas* (New York: Random House, 1974), 48–49.

75. Thomas, "Working Class Origins," 81.

76. Thurman, *Blacker the Berry,* 138–39.

77. Ralph Ellison and James McPherson, "Indivisible Man," *The Atlantic,* December 1970, p. 50. Malcolm X with Alex Haley, *The Autobiography of Malcolm X* (New York: Grove Press, 1964), 57.

CHAPTER THREE

1. Interview with Buddy Crew, Cleveland, Ohio, January 1980.

2. William Craig, "Recreational Activity Patterns in a Small Negro Urban Community: The Role of the Cultural Base," *Economic Geography* 48 (1972): 107–15.

3. Georgia Writers Project, WPA, *Drums and Shadows* (Athens: University of Georgia Press, 1940), 115; Marshall and Jean Stearns, *Jazz Dance* (New York: Macmillan, 1968), 235–38.

4. Kenneth Kusmer, *A Ghetto Takes Shape: Black Cleveland 1870–1930* (Urbana: University of Illinois Press, 1975), 58–59.

5. Russel B. Nye, "Saturday Night at the Paradise Ballroom: or Dance Halls in the Twenties," *Journal of Popular Culture* 7 (1973): 14, 16–17, 20. Louise de Koven Bowen, "Dance Halls," *The Survey,* June 3, 1911, p. 384. See also Leroy E. Bowman and Maria Ward Lambin, "Evidences of Social Relations as Seen in Types of New York City Dance Halls," *Journal of Social Forces* 3 (January 1925): 286–91; and Paul Cressey, *The Taxi-Dance Hall* (Chicago; University of Chicago Press, 1932).

6. *Cleveland Call and Post,* November 16, 1946; see also Russell Davis, *Black Americans in Cleveland: From George Peake to Carl B. Stokes, 1796–1969* (Washington: Associated Publishers, 1972), 310. Kusmer, *A Ghetto Takes Shape,* 180. *Cleveland Gazette,* August 17, 1912.

7. Interview with Charles Carr, Cleveland Ohio, January 1980.

8. Dominic J. Capeci, Jr., "Walter F. White and the Savoy Ballroom Controversy of 1943," *Afro-Americans in New York Life and History,* July 1981, pp. 16, 22.

9. Ibid., 19. See also Joe Bostic, "What's Behind the Savoy Closing?" *Peoples Voice* (New York), May 1, 1943, p. 3.

10. *The Cleveland Gazette,* November 6, 1909, January 14, 1905, announcements of Allegro Club–sponsored dance and installation of officers; January 20, 1912, announcement of Chauffers Club–sponsored third ball and leap year dance; June 17, 1911, announcement; A typical ad (from March 26, 1910) is illustrative:

> There will be an up to date dance every Monday evening at Halnorth's Hall (newly decorated) corner Woodland Avenue and East 55th Street, and you are cordially invited. Bring a friend. Goods order, good music, supper and refreshments served.
>
> Yours truly, Metropolitan Club.

11. Kusmer, *A Ghetto Takes Shape,* 100. Ads for the club's affairs were carried in the *Gazette.* One typical ad:

"Grand Annual Ball—Caterers Association at Tiffany's Dancing Hall 10300 Euclid Ave. —Monday evening June 8, 1914. Miss May Moores Orchestra—Admission 75 cents each" (*The Cleveland Gazette*, April 30, 1914). Monday evening was the night that most dance halls were reserved by and for blacks.

12. Jane Edna Hunter, *A Nickel and a Prayer* (Cleveland; Elli Kani Publishing, 1940), 68–69.

13. Frederick Rex, "Municipal Dance Halls," *National Civic Review*, July 1915, p. 417. *Cleveland Gazette*, November 12, 1910. Kusmer, *A Ghetto Takes Shape*, 49. See also "Dance Hall Inspections in Cleveland," *The Public*, November 22, 1912, p. 1123. "The Rev. John S. Rutldge, district supertenent of the Anti-Saloon League, talked on the 'Dangers and Duties of Citizenship', at Antioch Church, Monday evning and several of our ministers urged reform in the matter of Sunday dances, etc." (*The Cleveland Gazette*, December 3, 1914).

14. Jon M. Kingsdale, "The Poor Man's Club: Social Functions of the Urban Working Class Saloon," *American Quarterly* 25 (October 1973): 487.

15. Stearns, *Jazz Dance*, 95–96.

16. Rex, "Municipal Dance Halls," 419. "The Baker Administration of Cleveland," *National Municipal Review* 2 (January 1913): 464; see also "Dance Hall Law in Operation," *The Survey*, April 1, 1911; Julia Schoenfeld, "Commercial Recreation Legislation," *The Playground* 7 (March 1914): 461–71. Kusmer, *A Ghetto Takes Shape*, 49–50; see also Hunter, *A Nickel and a Prayer*, 131.

17. Davis, *Black Americans in Cleveland*, 143–45; Carr interview.

18. *Cleveland Gazette*, June 30, March 10, March 3, 1917.

19. Hunter, *A Nickel and a Prayer*, 123–24. *The Cleveland Gazette*, January 13, 1917. "The Cleveland Experiment," *The Outlook* 101 (August 24, 1912): 902. See

also "The Regulation of Dance Halls," *The Playground* 6 (December 1912): 342.

20. Malcolm X with Alex Haley, *The Autobiography of Malcolm X* (New York: Grove Press, 1964), 64.

21. Langston Hughes, "From the Big Sea," in *The New Negro Renaissance,* ed. Arthur P. Davis and Michael W. Peplow (New York: Holt, Rinehart and Winston, 1975), 177.

22. Interview with Jack Oliver, Cleveland, Ohio, January, 1980.

23. Kusmer, *A Ghetto Takes Shape,* 118–45.

24. Ibid., 146.

25. Davis, *Black Americans in Cleveland,* 20, 145.

26. "In Cleveland this mushroom growth, as regards its Negro population, achieved in the decade between 1910 and 1920 the phenomenal acceleration of three hundred per cent. Drawn from rural regions and villages by the lure of better wages, the Negroes like other underprivileged groups, offer a glaring mark for the rapacity of realtors and the dishonesty of politicians. . . . These 'black belts' quickly underwent degeneration, civic and fiscal, of a type known to virtually all American cities. Here was a golden opportunity for unscrupulous politicians; and greedily they seized upon it to serve their purposes, playing upon the ignorance of the Negro voter to entrench themselves in office, and then delivering the Negro over to every force of greed and vice which stalked around him" (Hunter, *A Nickel and a Prayer,* 120–21).

27. Carr interview. Christopher G. Wye, "Midwest Ghetto: Patterns of Negro Life and Thought in Cleveland, Ohio, 1929–1945" (unpublished dissertation, Kent State University, 1973), 25.

28. W. E. B. DuBois, *The Philadelphia Negro* (Millwood, N.Y.: Kraus, Thomson Organization, 1973), 311–12.

29. Kusmer, *A Ghetto Takes Shape,* 145. Interview with George Gould, vaudeville entertainer, Cleveland, Ohio, 1979.

30. Carr interview.

31. Interview with Jack Oliver, founding member, Twelve Counts Club; Cleveland, Ohio, December 1979.

32. St. Clair Drake and Horace R. Cayton, *Black Metropolis,* vol. 2 (New York: Harper & Row, 1962), 688.

33. Pyramid Club pictorial album in Charles L. Blockson Afro-American Collection, Temple University, Philadelphia.

34. Nye, "Saturday Night at the Paradise Ballroom," 21.

35. The phrase is from Drake and Cayton, *Black Metropolis,* vol. 2, 546.

36. "Shake Dancers, Their Private Life," *Our World* 9 (October 1953): 74–81.

37. Interview with U. S. Dearing, manager of the Cedar Gardens, Cleveland, Ohio, 1979.

38. Claude McKay, *Harlem: Negro Metropolis* (New York: Harcourt, Brace Jovanovich, 1940), 117–18; also William H. Jones, *Recreation and Amusement among Negroes in Washington, D.C.* (Washington, D.C.: Howard University Press, 1927), 131–34.

39. Dearing interview.

40. Wye, "Midwest Ghetto," 264. Dearing interview.

41. Ronald L. Morris, *Wait Until Dark* (Bowling Green, Ohio: Bowling Green University Popular Press, 1980), 32–33; Jones, *Recreation and Amusement,* 131–34.

42. McKay, *Harlem,* 113.

43. Drake and Cayton, *Black Metropolis,* 2:480. For examples of the prestige and power of policy men with respect to voting see Harold F. Gosnell, *Negro Politicians* (Chicago: University of Chicago Press, 1935) 136, 139, 140–42.

44. Carr interview. Clayton Fritchey, "Mayfield Mob Grabs Policy Racket Rule," *Cleveland Press,* October 18, 1938; Gosnell, *Negro Politicians,* 132.

45. Wye, "Midwest Ghetto," 234. *Cleveland Gazette,* November 19, 1933. Other estimates for Rufus Jones's in-

come and expenditures for "protection" were even larger, some as high as $12,000 per month.

46. Drake and Cayton, *Black Metropolis,* 2:478–94; see also J. Saunders Redding, "Playing the Numbers," *North American Review* 238 (December 1934): 534; Gosnell, *Negro Politicians,* 57–58, 173; McKay, *Harlem,* 110–11.

47. McKay, *Harlem,* 11–12; Redding, "Playing the Numbers," 534; David L. Lewis, *When Harlem Was in Vogue* (New York: Alfred A. Knopf, 1977), 220. Fritchey, "Mayfield Mob"; Wye, "Midwest Ghetto," 247–48; Carr interview.

48. Oliver interview. Wye, "Midwest Ghetto," 247–48.

49. *Cleveland Eagle,* May 8, 1936, May 15, 1936; Wye, "Midwest Ghetto," 245; *Cleveland Call and Post,* December 29, 1934, May 1936.

50. Oliver interview; Wye, "Midwest Ghetto," 263–64. "Confessions of a Numbers Banker," *Ebony,* July 1954, p. 60.

51. Interview with former club owner John H. "Chin" Ballard, January 1979, Cleveland, Ohio. "Black Type," *The Blood Horse* (1978), p. 5868.

52. Carr interview.

53. Gould interview, January 1980. Interview with James "Shortie" Adams, Cleveland, January 1980.

54. Adams interview.

55. Ballard interview.

56. Dearing interview.

57. Before running for council in 1944, Mrs. Capers had been an elementary school teacher. Contacts made at the PTA and through home visits during her lunch hour and after school acquainted her with the political ward. According to Mrs. Capers, these experiences taught her the importance of reaching the parents through the youngsters.

58. Interviews with Judge Jean Murrell Capers and

Jack Oliver, her campaign manager, January 1980, Cleveland, Ohio.

59. Capers interview.

60. "Newest Shuffle: The Madison," *Time,* April 4, 1960, p. 44. Structurally, the line and the circle were both surviving dance formats shared by many of the West African ethnic groups. As there are no surviving sacred African-American line dances, it is safe to assert that secularization of the line formation occurred earlier and more thoroughly. Accelerating that process was the fact that the African religious line dances in the plantation context shared a similar formation with the numerous secular European reels, in which men and women faced each other in lines. The Madison and the birdland of the 1950s, the continental of the 1960s, the bus stop of the 1970s, and the soul train line are clear examples of contemporary secular line formations. The circle, on the other hand, retained a sacred identity well into the twentieth century as the ring shout formation, most prominently observed along the South Carolina and Georgia coasts.

61. R. Lincoln Keiser, *The Vice Lords* (New York: Holt, Rinehart, Winston, 1969), 52.

62. Gerri Majors, *Black Society* (Chicago: Johnson Publishing, 1976); see also Stephen Birmingham, *Certain People* (Boston: Little, Brown, 1977). Both these works have excellent accounts of how the black elite spend their money; Majors's book gives a semihistorical account, which includes a look at the effect of the Depression on the elite community. Richard W. Thomas, "Working-Class Origins of Black Culture: Class Formation and the Division of Black Cultural Labor," *Minority Voices* 1 (Fall 1977): 81. E. Franklin Frazier, *Black Bourgeoisie* (New York: Macmillan Co., 1957), 11.

63. City records of Montgomery, Alabama, December 1856. See also Frederick Law Olmsted, *A Journey in the Seaboard Slave States* (New York: G. P. Putnam's Sons,

1904), 197. Samuel Mordecai, *Virginia Especially in By-Gone Days* (Richmond: West & Johnston Publishers, 1860), 350–57; Mary Boykin Chestnut, *A Diary from Dixie* (New York: D. Appleton & Company, 1905), entry for July 8–30, 1863, pp. 217–18.

64. DuBois, *Philadelphia Negro,* 225–28; C. V. Kiser, *Sea Island to City* (New York: Atheneum, 1969), 213–24.

65. Kusmer, *A Ghetto Takes Shape,* 98. Allan Spear, *Black Chicago* (Chicago: University of Chicago Press, 1967), 55, 71.

66. Kusmer, *A Ghetto Takes Shape,* 101–8; Spear, *Black Chicago,* 71–89. Julian Krawcheck, "Society Barred Negroes—They Formed Own Groups," *Cleveland Press,* May 30, 1963. Florette Henri, *Black Migration: Movement North 1900–1920* (New York: Anchor/Doubleday, 1976), 34.

67. Wye, "Midwest Ghetto," 329–30.

68. Interview with Susan Antoine, president, Cleveland chapter, Jack and Jill of America, January 1980, Cleveland, Ohio.

69. Nathan Hare, *Black Anglo-Saxons* (London: Collier Books, Collie Macmillan Ltd., 1965). See also Frazier, *Black Bourgeoisie,* 195–208.

70. Craig, "Recreational Patterns," 107–15.

71. Interview with Sondra Wilson, president of Tots and Teens, Cleveland chapter, January 1980, Cleveland, Ohio.

72. Hare, *Black Anglo-Saxons,* 87.

73. Wilson interview.

74. Roy Milton Clark, "Dance Party as a Socialization Mechanism," *Sociology and Sociological Research* 58 (1974): 145.

NOTES TO POSTSCRIPT

1. Zora Neale Hurston, "Characteristics of Negro Expressions," in *Negro Anthology,* ed. Nancy Cunard (New York: Negro Universities Press, 1969), 44.

2. "Style," *New York Times,* February 26, 1981, discusses eight of the newest night spots in New York City.

3. Interview with Jack Oliver, Cleveland, Ohio, January 1980.

4. Acklyn Lynch, "Culture on the Campus," *First World* 1 (May/June, 1977): 56. Cleaver's observation: "The stiff Mechanical Omnipotent Administrator and Ultra-feminines presented a startling spectacle as they entered in droves onto the dance floors to learn how to Twist" (Eldridge Cleaver, *Soul on Ice* [New York: Dell, 1968], 181).

5. These are undoubtedly European or American labels.

6. *New York Times,* January 24, 1982; see also Charles Jarmon, "The Sploe House: A Drinking Place of Lower Socio-Economic Status Negroes in a Southern City," *Black Experience: A Southern University Journal* 55 (June 1969): 53–61. The total number of shebeens for Bulawayo, Rhodesia, is estimated at around 450. See Harry Wolcott, *The African Beer Gardens of Bulawayo* (New Brunswick, N.J.: Rutgers Center of Alcohol Studies, 1984), 41–45, 227–28; Philip Mayer, *Xhosa in Town* (Cape Town: Oxford University Press, 1961), 111–12, 117–18. For a description of something similar to the African-American rent party see Joan May, *Drinking in a Rhodesian African Township* (Salisbury: University of Rhodesia, 1973), 23; also see D. H. Reader, *The Black Man's Portion* (Cape Town: Oxford University Press, 1961), 19, 82, 96, and 143.

7. For a discussion of the relevance of the colonial model for African-American culture, see Robert Staples, "Race and Colonialism: The Domestic Case in Theory and Practice," *Black Scholar,* June 1976, pp 37–48.

INDEX

Africa: call-and-response song patterns in music of, 45; dance in (*see* Traditional dance, African); influence of, on political institutions in America, 42–43; as inspiration for modern dance, 174, 175–76

African-American(s): benevolent societies (nineteenth century), 68–72, 74; education, 69, 166; elites (*see* Elites, African-American); emerging culture of, 21–22, 47; migration of, to urban areas, 64, 73, 94, 136–37, 158, 164–65; oratory tradition among, 72; politicians, 130–31, 135–37; sexual liasons between whites and, in New Orleans, 52–61; sociocultural identity of, linked to dance, 117–19;

terrorism against, 73. *See also* Slave(s)

African-American dance culture, ix–xii, 173–76; block parties, 154–62; in cabarets, 142–52; competitions in, 116–17, 157–58; as covert social activity, 76–77; disco and, 174–75; elite dance forms, 70, 74–76, *102*, *110*, 170; emergence of, 15–21; as expression of independence, 4, 13, 15, 46–48, 173; influence of African dance on (*see* Traditional dance, African); insurrectionary aspects of, on plantations, 22, 31–35, 37–38, 46–47; jook houses, honky-tonks, and after-hours joints, 76–94; in membership club dance halls, 135, 137–41;

African-American dance culture (*cont.*):
in municipal dance halls, 122–23, 129–30, 133–34; of nineteenth-century benevolent societies, 69–70, 71, *102*; northern vs. southern, 117; rent parties, chittlin' struts, and blue Monday affairs, 94–119; sacred and secular aspects, on plantations, 15–19; under slavery (*see* Slavery, social dancing under); standardization of, after emancipation, 67–69, 81–82
After-hours joints, 78, 88–93, *109*, 173, 176; rent shouts as temporary, 98, 111
Albion-Frigate (ship), 10
Alcoholic beverages: at cabaret parties, 153; in cabarets, 149; in honky-tonks, 85, 86; in Kenya, 175; in membership clubs, 137, 138; on plantations, 23, 28–29; at rent shouts, 98, 111; on slave ships, 7, 12; at urban public slave dances, 41
American Guild of Variety Artists (AGVA), 150–51
American society: African-American dance and, xi; access of nineteenth-century blacks to, 70, 75; adoption of black dance/music by, 93, 174
Angelou, Maya, 116–17
Animal characters in music, 45–46
Anti-Saloon League, 128
Apex Club, Cleveland, Ohio, 139
Appomattox Club, 74
Ashanti culture, 40, 159
Asymmetry as balance in dance, 18, 20

Baker, Newton D., 129
Balance, asymmetry in, 18, 20
Ballard, John H., 149
Baltimore, Maryland, 154
Bambara culture, 79–80
Barbot, James, 10
Barran, Pedro, 56
Barrelhouse joints, 88
Barrow, David C., Jr., 44
Bartholomew, Robert O., 130
Basie, Count, 133
Beer dance, 28–29
Bembe dance parties, 16–17
Benevolent societies, post-emancipation, 68–72, 74, *102*, *106*, *107*, *108*, 135. *See also* Membership clubs
Big apple (dance), 81
Billy Kersands sextette, 90

Birdland (dance), 158

Black bottom (dance), 67, 83, 87, 93, 116

Black Dance (Emery), xii

Blackman, Teddy, 144

Black Metropolis (Cayton, Drake), 140

Blake, Eubie, 111

Block parties, 154–62; in Cleveland, Ohio, 154–58; dance competitions in, 157–58; dancing at, 158–60; music, 156; as vent for community hostilities, 160–62

Blue Grass Club, Cleveland, Ohio, 149

Blue Monday affairs, 94

Blues music, 77, 83, 86

Bonquet, José, 56

Bop (dance), 158

Bootlegging, 146

Bowen, Louise deKoven, 124

Boyd, Albert "Starlight," 128, 131, 136–37

Brazil, African-American culture in, 30

Break dancing, 20

Breakdown (dance), 19

Brookes (ship), 7

Brown, James, 78

Bryd, Nancy, 48

Buffet flats, 89–90

Business, African-American, 89, 91–92; cabarets, 143, 146–50

Buzzard (dance), 116

Buzzard lope (dance), 19, 40, 83, 116

Cabaret(s), 89, *109*, 142–54, 173; in Cleveland, 144–45, 147, 149–50; dancing in, 145; decline of, 150–52; factors in emergence of black-owned, 143, 146–50; lotteries conducted in, 146–50; origins, 142–43; racial segregation in white, 143–45; tax on, 151–52; unionization of entertainers in, 150–51. *See also* After-hours joints

Cabaret party, 152–53, 175

Cakewalk (dance), 19, 67, 87

Call-and-response songs, 44–46

Camel (dance), 116

Camel walk (dance), 159

Campbell, Elen, 52

Capers, Jean Murrell, 154–55

Carr, Charles, 137

Castle, Vernon and Irene, 93

Caterers Association, 165

Caterers Club, 74

Cayton, Horace R., 140

Cedar Gardens cabaret, Cleveland, Ohio, 144–45

Chaney, Mack, 30

Charleston (dance), 19, 67, 83, 116, 158

Charleston, South Carolina, 35; slave balls, 51
Charley of the Pinkster Hill, 41–42
Chicago Defender (newspaper), 73, 154
Chicago, Illinois, 73, 74, 154; policy drawings in, 147–48
Chittlin' circuit, 82
Chittlin' strut, 94, 113
Christianity, 15, 19
Christmas, dancing on plantations during, 22–26
Church, African-American, 67, 75; dances sponsored by, 127, 132; origins of rent parties in socials at, 96
Clarkson, Thomas, 6–7
Cleaver, Eldridge, 175
Cleveland, Ohio, ix; before 1917, 73, 74; block parties in, 154–58; cabarets in, 144–45, 147, 149–50; crime and cabaret policy rackets in, 148–49; elite affairs in, 164–66, 168–70; housing exploitation in, 95, 115; membership clubs in, 135–40; municipal dance halls in, 125, 126–32, 134; policy drawings in, 147–48; politicians in, 130–31, 135–37
Clubs. *See* Benevolent societies, post-emancipation; Membership clubs

Code of silence among slaves, 65–66
Collins, Robert, 26–27
Commercial-urban entertainment complex, xi, 121–71; block parties, 154–62; elite social affairs, 162–71; membership clubs, 135–41; night clubs, show bars, and cabarets, 142–54; public/municipal dance halls, 121–34
Concert saloon, 124–25
Cooke, Sam, 78
Coquet, Bernardo, 56–57
Corn shucking/husking activities, 43–46
Cotillions and debutante balls, 162, 167–71
Cotton gin, 21
Crawford, John, 28
Crowe, Eyre, 51
Cuba, African-American dance culture in, 16, 30, 40, 65
Cutting contests: dance, 116–17, 157–58; music, 90–91, 111

Dance. *See* African-American dance culture
Dance halls, membership club. *See* Membership clubs
Dance halls, public and municipal, 121–34, 173; in Cleveland, Ohio, 125, 126–27, 130–32; community

significance of, 129, 132–34; dance forms found in, 122–23, 129–30; integration in, 126–27; movement against saloon-style, 128–29; one-night affairs, 125–26, 132–33; origins of, 124–25; politics and, 123–24, 130–31, 134; school auditoriums as, 131–32; segregation in, 123, 125–26, 132; types, 124–25

Dance of Africa, The (Warren), 3

"Dancing the slaves" on slave ships, 6–13; to entertain slavers, 9–11; for health purposes, 6–7; music for, 8–9; slaves' view of, 9; techniques for, 11–12; white participation in, 10–11

Debutante balls and cotillions, 162, 167–71

Depression, great, 97, 115, 139

Detroit, Michigan, 74

Dia de Reyes celebration, 40

Disco, 174–75

Dorsey, Thomas A., 78

Douglass, Frederick, 31, 65, 71

Douglass Club, Cleveland, Ohio, 150

Drake, St. Clair, 140

Drums, 30, 33, 65–66, 71

Du Bois, W. E. B., 138

Eastern Star, 68

Education of African-Americans, 69, 166

Election day celebrations, 42

Elites, African-American, 162–71; adoption of white culture by, 70, 74–75, 162, 163–64, 167; alienation of, from core black culture, 117–19, 162–63, 174; benevolent society affairs, 69–70, 74–75, 163–64, 167; cabaret patronage by, 145–46; characteristics of, 164–66; cotillions and debutante balls, 162, 167–71; dance forms adopted by, 70, 74–76, *102, 110,* 170; dinner dances, 162, 167; membership clubs, 74, 140–41, 165–66; race uplift sponsored by, 69–70, 75, 163, 167; slave balls, 48–49, 163

Elks club, 68, 74, 135

Ellington, Duke, 111

Ellison, Ralph, 118

Emancipation, changes in black life brought by, 66–73

Emancipation Day celebrations, 70–72

Emery, Lynne, xii

Employment, African-American, 97–98, 115–16, 122

Entertainers, unionization of, 150–51
Erenberg, Lewis, xii
Euchre Club, 74

Family life under slavery, 24, 64–65
Fish tail (dance), 83
Fleming, Thomas, 130–31, 135–37
Folk medicine, 19
Foxtrot (dance), 129
Franklin, Aretha, 78
Frazier, E. Franklin, 162
Free African Society of Philadelphia, 68
Free African Union Society of Providence, Rhode Island, 68
Free blacks: restrictions on, after emancipation, 66–67; restrictions on, during slavery, 55; status of, in black slave communities, 48; urban dance celebrations performed by, during slavery, 35–43
Funky butt (dance), 83, 84

Gambling: in cabarets, 146–50; in honky-tonks, 85, 86; at membership clubs, 135; at rent shouts, 98
Gangs, urban street, 161–62
Gayarre, Charles, 52
Gaye, Marvin, 78

Gazette, The (newspaper), 125, 132
Gens de couleur, 54
Georgia (ship), 10–11
Georgia hutch (dance), 67
Gilliat, Sy, 48
Good-time flats, 89
Gospel music, 78
Gould, George, 97
Grand United Order of True Reformers, 68
Grant, Coot, 87–88
Greene, Al, 78
Grind (dance), 83
Group dancing, breakdown of, and change to individual/partnered dance, 81, 93

Hager, Steven, xii
Hairdos, influence on dance forms, 92–93
Hare, Nathan, 170
Herskovits, Melville, 40, 84
Hicks and Sawyers Georgia Minstrels, 90
Hines, Ike, 90
Hip Hop (Hager), xii
Hodge, Frank, 148, 149
Holidays: dancing on plantations during, 22–26, 31; urban slave dancing during, 39–43
Honky-tonks, 83, 84–88, 173
Hoodoo, 19
Horse (dance), 158

House shouts, 94
Housing: exploitation in, 94–96, 115; ghettoization of, 115
Howe, George, 7
Hughes, Langston, 133, 141
Hunter, Jane Edna, 128, 132, 136
Hurston, Zora Neal, 63, 79, 82–83

Impressions, The, 78
Individual/partnered dance, breakdown of group dance to, 81, 93
Instruments. See Musical instruments
Insurrectionary aspects of slave dances, 22, 31–35, 37–38, 46–47
Integration in municipal dance halls, 126–27
Itch (dance), 83, 84

Jacobs, Harriet Brent, 39
Jazz, 83, 86
Jazz Dance (Stearns), xii
Jerk (dance), 19, 78
Jerry Rescue Day, 70–71
John Canoe festival, 39–40
Johnson, James P., 111
Johnson, John B., 148, 149, 150
Jones, Charles C., 65
Jones, Rufus, 148, 149

Jook: defined, 63, 76, 79–80; on plantations, 78–79, 105
Jook continuum, x; dance in transition era prior to jook, 63–76; development of jook houses, honky-tonks, and after-hours joints, 76–94; rent parties, chittlin' struts, and blue Monday affairs, 94–119
Jook houses, 76, 79, 80–84, 103, 104, 107, 110; dances in, 83–84; decline of, 94, 173; influence on cabarets, 143; influence on membership club dancing, 141
Jukebox, 101, 112
Juneteenth celebration, 72

Keiser, R. Lincoln, 161–62
Kenya, 175
King, B. B., 84
Knight, Gladys, 78
Knights and Daughters of I Will Rise, 68

Le Page du Pratz, Antoine Simon, 37–38
Legal restrictions: on dance halls, 129; miscegenation, 61, 62; musical instruments, 32, 33; racial segregation, 54–56; quadroon balls, 53
Lindy hop (dance), 84, 133, 158

Little Richard, 78
Locke, Alain, 141
Log Cabin cabaret, Cleveland, Ohio, 149–50
Lonardo, "Big Angelo," 148
Lone Star Race Pride, Friendship, Love and Help, Order of, 68
Lottery activities in cabarets, 146–50
Louisiana, African-American dance in slavery days of, 53–61

Madison (dance), 158
Malcolm X, 118, 133
Manasseh Society, 74
Maschke, Maurice, 136
Mashed potatoes (dance), 78, 158
Mason, Benny, 149
Masons, 68, 69, 74
Mayfield Road boys, Cleveland, Ohio, 148–49
Membership clubs, 135–41, 173; alcoholic beverages in, 137, 138; backing from political parties, 135–41; dances sponsored by, at club halls, 135, 137–41; dances sponsored by, at white-owned dance halls, 127–28; fees, 139; politicians, political patronage, and, 135–37; post-emancipation societies, 68–

72, 74, *102, 106, 107, 108*; as transition from jook houses, 141
Messaround (dance), 116
Middle passage. *See* Slave ships
Migration to urban areas, African-American, 64, 73, 94, 136–37, 158, 164–65
Milking the cow (dance step), 122
Miro, Estevan, 55
Miscegenation, 49–50; legal restrictions on, 61, 62; *placage* system, 53, 58–61
Mixed-race population in slavery era, 49–50, 52–53; *gens de couleur* in Louisiana, 54, 55
Mobile, Alabama, 35
Monday night affairs, 125–26, 132–33
Monjetta, Alston, 23
Monkey glide (dance), 129–30
Mordacai, Jimmy, 20
Mordecai, Samuel, 48–49
Morton, Jelly Roll, 85
Music: at block parties, 156; in cabarets, 145, 146; cutting contest competitions, 90–91, 111; honky-tonk, 84–85, 86; jook, 82–83; jukebox, *101*, 112; in plantation culture, 14, 24, 27, 29–31; prerecorded, 112,

156; relationship of modern secular and sacred, 77–79; at rent parties, 111–12; on slave ships, 8–9. *See also* Sacred dance and music; Secular dance and music; Songs

Musical instruments, 24, 29–31; drums, 30, 33, 65–66, 71; in jook houses, 83; laws forbidding, 32, 33; susa, 30

New England, election day celebrations, 42–43

New Orleans, Louisiana, 35, 38; sexual relations between whites and mixed-race individuals in, 52–54

Newspapers, black, 73

New York: after-hours clubs in, 90; dance halls in Harlem, 126–27; Jerry Rescue Day in, 70–71; Pinkster celebration in, 40–42; rent parties in Harlem, 111, 114

Night clubs. *See* Cabaret(s)

North Carolina, John Canoe festival in, 39–40

Numbers drawings in cabarets, 146–50

Nye, Russel, 124–25

Oak and Ivy Club, 74

Ocha party, 16

Octoroon, The: Or Life in Louisiana, 55

Odd Fellows, 68, 69, 74

Old Settlers Club, 74

Oliver, Jack, 150

Olmstead, Frederick Law, 16–17; on *placage* system, 58–59

Oratory tradition, 72

"Party for the gods" dance parties, 16–17, 77

Pay parties, 118–19

Pearson, Horace, 150

Pennington, Ann, 93

Perry, Mary C. "Diamond Tooth," 149

Philadelphia, Pennsylvania, 154; membership clubs, 140

Philadelphia Negro, The (Du Bois), 138

Phyllis Wheatley Association, 132

Pickens, Buster, 88

Pierpont, John, 23–24

Pigeon wing (dance), 19

Pinkster celebration, 40–42

Placage (placee) system, 53, 58–61

Plantation(s), 13–47; alcoholic beverages used, 23, 28–29; corn husking activities, 43–46; dancing as insurrection, 22, 31–35, 37–38; derision of whites

Plantation(s) (*cont.*):
through dance/song, 46–
47; emergence of African-
American culture, 21–22,
47; holiday dancing, 22–
26, 28, 31, 39–43; jooking
on, 78–79, *105*; musical
instruments, 29–31; secu-
lar vs. sacred dancing, 15–
19; survival of African culture, 13–14; types of
dances performed, 19–21;
urban public dances vs.
dances on, 35–43; weekend
dancing, 26–27, 38; white
attendance at slave dances
on, 51–52; white attitudes
toward slave culture and
dance on, 14–15, 22, 27,
28, 32–33, 37–38, 47;
work patterns and slave culture, 14–15, 19, 21–22,
43–46
Poe, Samuel, 28–29
Police presence at dances, *99*
Policy lotteries in cabarets,
146–50
Politics and patronage:
cabarets and, 148, 149; existence of dance halls linked
to, xi, 123–24, 130–31,
134
Pop (dance), 123
Pop locking (dance), 19
Poppin' the hips (dance), 158.
See also Snake hips (dance)

Powdermaker, Hortense, 86
Praise houses, 18
Price, Roger, 149
Prince Hall Masons, 69
Prohibition, 138, 139, 148
Pyramid Club, Philadelphia,
Pennsylvania, 140–41

Quadroon balls, 53–54, 57–
58, 61–62

R&C Chatterbox Club, Cleveland, Ohio, 149–50
"Race men," 72
Racial uplift concept, dance
and, 69–70, 74–75, 118,
163, 167
Rap Attack, The (Toop), xii
Reconstruction era, 63–76;
changes in rural black life
after emancipation, 66–73;
development of jook during,
81–82; functions of black
culture prior to, 63–66; migration to urban areas after
(*see* Migration to urban
areas, African-American)
Reform movements against
dance halls, 127–29
Religion. *See* Church, African-
American; Sacred dance and
music
Rent parties, 94–119, 173;
advertising and tickets for,
113–15; black so-
ciocultural identity and

dancing at, 117–19; cutting contests in, 90–91; dancing at, 116–17; decline of, 115–16; employment problems and, 97; exploitation in housing and, 94–96; food at, 113; origins of, 96; pay parties, 118–19; temporary after-hours rent shouts, 98, 111

Republican Club, Cleveland, Ohio, 135, 137, 138

Richardson, Willie, 148, 149, 150

Ring shout (dance), 81

Rock (dance), 122

Royal Vagabonds, 166

Royster, Earl, 98

Sacred dance and music: development of jook format from, 77, 81; on plantations, 15–19; relationship of modern secular music to, 77–79; scratching gestures in African, 83–84; on slave ships, 3–4, 12

St. Louis, Missouri, 39

Salem, Massachusetts, election day celebrations, 42–43

Samaritans, 68

Sand (dance), 116

Savoy Ballroom, Harlem, 126–27

Schoenfeld, Julia, 132

School auditoriums, dances in, 131–32

Secular dance and music: modern sacred music and, 77–79; on plantations, 15–19; urban, in slavery era, 35–43, 50–62. *See also* Commercial-urban entertainment complex; Jook continuum

Segregation, 54–56; in cabarets, 143–45; in housing, 115; in municipal dance halls, 123, 125–26, 132

Set de flo' (dance), 19, 20

Sexuality and dance, 87–88, 89–90, 93

Sexual relations, interracial, 49–50; initiated at slave balls, 52–54; *placage* system, 53, 58–61

Shebeen, 175–76

Shimmy (dance), 83, 87, 116

Shines, Johnny, 79

Shout forms, 19, 79; dance, 78; ceremonies, 16–17; ring, 81

Show bars. *See* Cabaret(s)

Sisters of the Mysterious Ten, 68

Skate (dance), 116

Skin color and social status, 50, 74, 75

Slave(s): code of silence, 65–66; dance as independent

Slave(s) (*cont.*):
cultural expression among, 4, 13, 15; insurrectionary aspects of dance among, 22, 31–35, 37–38, 46–47; plantation holiday privileges, 23–24; status distinctions, 48–50; treatment of, on slave ships, 4–13; viewpoint of, on slave-ship dancing, 9. *See also* African-American dance culture; Plantation(s)
Slave owner(s): attitudes of, toward slave culture and dance, 4, 5–6, 14–15, 18, 19, 22, 27, 28, 32–33, 37–38, 47; derision of, in slave dance/song, 46–47; slave dancing as entertainment for, 9–10
Slave rebellions, 32–33, 34
Slavery, social dancing under, 3–62; community and culture fostered by, 63–66; on plantations, 13–47; on slave ships, 3–13; urban slave balls, 48–62
Slave ships, 3–13; "dancing the slaves" on, 6–13; philosophies of loading, 5, 6; role of dance among African captives on, 3–4
Slop (dance), 84, 158
Slow drag (dance), 83, 88
Smallpox ordinances, 66

Smith, Bessie, 90
Smith, William B., 28
Smith, Willie (the Lion), 111
Snake hips (dance), 67, 83, 84, 122–23, 158
Social Circle club, 74
Somerset County, Maryland, 39
Songs: call-and-response, 44–46; plantation work, 14; on slave ships, 8–9
"Sorrows of Yamba, The; Or, the Negro Woman's Lamentation," 9
South Africa, 175–76
South Carolina, slave rebellions in, 32–33, 34
Staple Singers, 78
Starlight Café, Cleveland, Ohio, 136
Stearns, Jean, xii, 87
Stearns, Marshall, xii, 87
Steppin' Out (Erenberg), xii
Stono Rebellion, 32–33, 34
Street gangs at block parties, 161–62
Suncho dance party, 16
Susa (musical instrument), 30
Suso, Foday Musa, 30

Tap dancing, 20, 84
Tax, cabaret, 151–52
Television, effect on cabarets, 152